C000201627

CYBERPUNK

First published in Great Britain 2000 by Pocket Essentials, 18 Coleswood Road, Harpenden, Herts, AL5 1EQ

Distributed in the USA by Trafalgar Square Publishing, PO Box 257, Howe Hill Road, North Pomfret, Vermont 05053

A CIP catalogue record for this book is available from the British Library.

ISBN 1-903047-28-5

9 8 7 6 5 4 3 2 1

Book typeset by Pdunk
Printed and bound by Cox & Wyman

To Mark, for having a mercy to be thrown on.

Acknowledgements

Thanks as always to the Prefab Four for friendship and support, and to Tanya Brown for the Prom tickets, the futon and trips to a sea that was wet and moved; much needed distractions from a very tight schedule. Andrew Macrae made me think about the Pacific Rim and racism and has been a good sounding board. Istvan Csicsery-Ronay Jr offered some helpful advice on my outline, and saved me a few times from myself. Thanks to Farah Mendlesohn (who mentioned the possibility of this book), Edward James, Tanya Brown and Paul and Elizabeth Billinger for letting me raid their book and video collections. The biggest thanks of all go to Mark Bould, as selfless supplier of dozens of books, buyer of rounds (sometimes with his own money...), massager of ego, booker of hotel rooms, and as co-worker and comrade.

CONTENTS

1. Introduction

What you are holding in your hand is already an obsolete product. It's also the first time it's been a tangible object in the process of its creation. The neurones of thought trigger spasmodic movements of digits (an unavoidable meat medium) onto keys, which is converted electronically into 0s and 1s stored on the C drive of my PC. The zeroes and ones, representing words, are eventually sent via e-mail to the publisher, who uses a computer to 'typeset' these words and – having sent me a PDF to proof-read – sends them to the printers. It is only then the words hit paper, and this is almost a shame, since the actual is always disappointing compared to the virtual version. And the cheque which is my payment goes straight into a bank account without my ever seeing anything recognisable as money. In fact, Pocket Essentials could have transferred this sum to my account direct. You may have ordered this book from a website and paid by credit card. Certainly its position will have been tracked by computer at some point in its route through wholesale and retail.

Think how much computers impinge upon our lives: clocks, watches, calculators, PCs, MACs, any time we buy something, virtually every time we write a letter or pay a bill. Traffic lights. The Underground and Rail Networks. The National Lottery. Air traffic control. E-mail. Computer games. Every phone call. As the clocks in each time zone flicked from 23:59.59 on 31 December 1999 to 00:00.00 on 1 January 2000 the world held its breath: not only that the champagne would be fine, but also that the computers would still be working. International economics teetered on the edge of collapse thanks to decisions about computer chip design taken in the 1970s.

*

Let us try to understand cyberpunk via economics.

The medieval world economy was a mixture of barter and coinage. So many pigs were worth so many bags of grain. The coins were worth the amount of precious metal which made them up. Western countries were emerging as nation states, with a strict hierarchical – feudal – structure in most.

The modern world – for the sake of argument from the late fifteenth century – saw nations competing with each other on a greater scale than before, and the establishment of empires across the world: by the dawn of the twentieth century Africa, South America, Australasia and parts of southern Asia had been carved up between half a dozen European nations. Trade was international, and began involving paper currency as a kind of

IOU backed by gold reserves in various banks across Europe and in the USA. Capitalism had taken over from feudalism; the aristocracy and royalty of Europe dwindled in influence, to be replaced by a class of businessmen – part of an emerging middle-class – and the workers who staffed the factories.

In the twentieth century, the situation changed again, especially after the Second World War. One by one the colonies had sought, had taken or occasionally had been granted their independence, and the rôle of the nation decreased in world power as the numbers increased. What took the nation's place were corporations who thought on a global scale, cutting across national boundaries: a company might have factories in Europe and Asia and markets in America and Europe. Whereas in the nineteenth century France, Britain and Germany competed for Africa, today Microsoft, News International, Coca Cola, Time Warner, Nike and a number of other multinational corporations with turnovers greater than many small countries compete for world domination. The Pound and the Dollar are no longer backed by gold, but supported by a kind of collective consensus as to their value. In fact, money increasingly becomes an illusion, with wages going direct into bank accounts and out again to pay for products without ever being in our pockets: the money is just ones and zeroes on the computers of the banking corporations. Banks keep our money in cyberspace, computer memory and networks, not vaults.

Of course, for some industries it was all but impossible to avoid operating across national boundaries. From its origins in the 1920s, radio was seen as both an invasive medium of foreign propaganda, and a useful means of disseminating national characteristics abroad. The development of satellites allowed radio, television and telecommunications to spread across the world. In parallel to this, a series of wire networks grew – ostensibly to allow military communications in the event of a war, and this technology allowed academics to communicate with each other via their computers. This evolved into the Internet, a global, virtual community.

In the last 30 or so years, the economic emphasis of the world seemed to shift from Europe and North America to the Pacific Rim: the tiger economies of Asia began to dominate, with exports of electronic equipment, cars and so on to the West, as well as their stock exchanges becoming increasingly important. The Japanese, in particular, seemed to be conquering the West by economics. And with the dissolution of the old 'evil' Soviet empire, perhaps there was here a new enemy for America to face... and a chance to tell some new stories.

Cyberpunk

In the late 1970s and early 1980s a number of writers wished to explore this brave new world, using science fiction as its means. The most visible example of this was William Gibson, whose novel *Neuromancer* (1984) won the Hugo Award (given by sf fans) and the Nebula Award (given by sf writers) for the best sf novel of the year. Gibson depicted a near-future world dominated by computer networks and Japanese corporations, with artificially intelligent entities possibly running things behind the scenes. He could write with such poetry about computers, because at the time he knew little about them: to him a modem was an exotic piece of equipment.

Gibson had published a number of short stories prior to this, and these led to him being labelled as a writer of Cyberpunk by the editor and critic Gardner Dozois. Dozois linked Gibson with Bruce Sterling, Rudy Rucker, John Shirley, and Lewis Shiner as authors of a science fiction set in a near future, dominated by high technology including computers, computer networks and human/machine hybrids. The technology provided the *cyber* part of the label; the street life of the stories and novels offered the *punk* part.

But Dozois was not the first to use the term; credit for this is taken by Bruce Bethke, whose story 'Cyberpunk' was published in *Amazing* in 1983 having circulated in manuscript for some time beforehand. It is possible that the term predated even him; certainly the roots of cyberpunk itself can be traced back into the history of sf and literature in general.

Science Fiction

Science fiction is a genre of popular fiction, which has been produced in a number of media: written, visual and aural. Sf has roots in European literature, and the use of imaginary lands to comment upon contemporary issues can be found at least as far back as Plato's *Republic*. It was only with the rise of the realist novel, in the second half of the eighteenth century, that fantastical fiction became distinguished from general literature. The most obvious form of fantastic fiction of the period was the Gothic novel, and a pertinent late example of this was Mary Shelley's *Frankenstein, or The Modern Prometheus* (1818), where recent medical speculations upon the nature of life were used to update the golem myth. In the 1890s, H G Wells wrote a number of what he termed 'scientific romances,' where science again replaced magic as the driving force behind his narratives. *The Time Machine* (1895) and *The War Of The Worlds* (1898) both drew upon evolutionary theory, as well as astronomy and other sciences.

He was not alone, as many other writers of the turn of the century wrote works of proto-sf, such as Robert Louis Stevenson, Jack London and Joseph Conrad & Ford Madox Ford.

But these were also writers of books which were respected. Sf as a genre grew up in the pulp magazines of the 1920s and it has been predominantly produced by writers from the United States. The term as used today developed from 'scientifiction,' a word coined by Hugo Gernsback the editor of *Amazing Stories*, April 1926, to describe: 'the Jules Verne, H G Wells and Edgar Allan Poe kind of story – a charming romance intermingled with scientific fact and prophetic vision.'

Gernsback saw sf as a form that would be informed by science, but this shouldn't be taken to mean that sf is merely predictive. Sf can equally use science (in the broadest sense) as a device with which to examine the present. Sf poses the question 'What if?' One form of the question is to examine the impact of new technology upon a society, and the behaviour of its inhabitants. Another is to suggest a possible revision or advancement in scientific knowledge, and extrapolate the way the world would change. Finally an alternate course of historical events might be suggested. In practice sf can employ different combinations of the question.

An increasing number of professional sf writers began to be published in magazines such as *Amazing* and *Astounding Stories*, the latter edited by sf writer John W Campbell Jr. At that time, most sf took the form of short stories or novellas in magazines, which could then be linked together in book form; one example is Asimov's *Foundation* trilogy (1942-58) which tells the story of a predicted collapse of the galactic empire, and the establishment of foundations to bring about the inevitable new galactic order. Predictions – and their limitations – were at the heart of the sequence.

Since sf was a fiction led by ideas, scientific or otherwise, matters of characterisation and style were often ignored. Indeed, since writers wrote in the white hot heat of inspiration, a second draft was a rarity. In the 1950s, this began to change with the emergence of a number of writers who could combine the three elements. Theodore Sturgeon, Robert Sheckley, Alfred Bester and Philip K Dick, among others, brought a new wit and maturity to the form, under the tutelage of editors such as Anthony Boucher (*Fantasy And Science Fiction*) and Horace Gold (*Galaxy*).

Alfred Bester is best-known in this context for his novel *Tiger! Tiger!* (1956, variant title and text *The Stars My Destination*, 1957) which features the character Gulliver Foyle. Foyle is marooned on a spaceship and escapes by jaunting – teleporting – to asteroids inhabited by tattooed men. He vows vengeance on the spaceship Vorga, which failed to rescue him.

This character can leap from place to place, facilitating a speedy plot and demanding constant invention from Bester, and he provides it – although the English town names used for characters may be distracting to British readers. On several occasions Bester experimented with typography, having letters spill across the page.

Philip K Dick was an influence from at least three directions: in his own right, from the adaptation of a novel into the film *Blade Runner* (1982) and from his suspected influence upon Thomas Pynchon, who in turn influenced the cyberpunks. *Do Androids Dream Of Electric Sheep?* (1968) is probably his best-known work, featuring Rick Deckard, a bounty hunter assigned to track down and destroy a number of escaped androids. Since the androids are very close to being human themselves, they might almost be thought of as cyborgs; certainly the human characters who dial up their emotions on a Mood Organ should be thought of as cyborgs. Dick's post-holocaust settings, anti-heroes and seat-of-the-pants plotting all form an influence upon cyberpunk. Dick was never one for narratives involving computer users (although the distinctly below par *Vulcan's Hammer* (1960) features two super computers), but he did show a distrust of big business that cyberpunks were to echo.

Meanwhile, in Britain, a group of writers centred on *New Worlds* and its editor Michael Moorcock had become tired with the clichés of bug-eyed monsters and outer space; they wanted to explore the inner space landscapes of psychology and the media. Brian Aldiss (*Report On Probability A* (1968)), Norman Spinrad (*Bug Jack Barron* (1969)), J G Ballard (*The Atrocity Exhibition* (1970)) and others did just that, with some financial backing from the Arts Council of Great Britain.

J G Ballard became the great writer of the period, with his near-future catastrophe novels, demonstrating that sf need not consist of mad scientists and their beautiful daughters, nor of blond, blue-eyed, square-jawed heroes who can conquer the galaxy single-handedly. What mattered was not the technology itself – the motor car in *Crash* (1973), say – but its impact on those who used it. The media landscape depicted by Ballard – his sense that in the 1960s we were living inside an sf novel – has developed exponentially during the last 40 years.

John Brunner was another writer on the edge of the New Wave, who wrote 4 great novels about the end of the world: *Stand On Zanzibar* (1968, overpopulation) *The Jagged Orbit* (1969, the military industrial complex and the Mafia), *The Sheep Look Up* (1972, pollution) and *The Shockwave Rider* (1975, featuring a computer virus, as well as the media landscape). Brunner's fragmented style – featuring a sense of the cinematic, quotations, newspaper clippings – was a homage to the American modernist John Dos Passos and his novel *USA* (1930-1936). The remorselessly downbeat nature of the novels was an undoubted influence upon cyberpunk.

Back in America, black sf writer Samuel R Delany was rewriting the possibilities of sf. Most notably *Babel-17* (1966) featured a spaceship into which the pilot could be plugged as a cyborg, and concerned itself with an imagined language. Delany was a great stylist and experimenter; his most successful experiment both in terms of critical reception and sales figures was *Dhalgren* (1975). An unnamed narrator arrives in a near-future city, and encounters a number of residents before leaving again, having written a novel that may be *Dhalgren*. The crossover success of Delany showed that writers could have vast sales outside of sf as well as within it.

The new waves of sf in Britain and America showed the possibility of authors dealing with real-world politics head-on. Joanna Russ' *The Female Man* (1975), published half a decade after being written, explored the treatment of women and made uncomfortable reading for some, but rightly became a classic. Towards the end of the novel, Jael has sex with a man – an event which causes surprise and even disgust given the matriarchal nature of the societies depicted. But Davy is no ordinary man, he is a cyborg, with a chimpanzee's brain, wired to have sex at her whim; this could well be the earliest example of technodildonics in sf. Russ' Alyx narratives *Picnic On Paradise* (1968) and *Alyx* (1976)/*The Adventures Of Alyx* (1987) offered adventure narratives with strong women who were not just male objects of desire or power fantasies. Gibson was to use the name Jael in his early novels, presumably in some kind of homage. Alice Sheldon, writing under her pseudonym James Tiptree Jr, produced another work of proto-cyberpunk in 'The Girl Who Was Plugged In' (1973), in which a 17-year-old girl from the streets is electronically augmented and turned into a walking advertisement.

Despite many significant novels being published in the 1970s – the tail end of the British New Wave and the early writings of authors who would emerge fully in the 1980s - the 1970s seems to be a decade of shrinkage within sf, at least written sf. Even the unprecedented box-office success of filmed sf in the shape of *Star Wars* (1977) seemed to be a retrograde step, taking the naïve sensibility of 50-year-old sf as a model. In Britain there was no regular sf magazine between the collapse of *New Worlds* in the mid-1970s and *Science Fiction Monthly* (1974-1976) and the establishment of *Interzone* in 1982. The world was changing – the old order of presidents like Nixon gave way to someone who had made a living as an actor, international politics was changing as the Communist Bloc tried to hold on to power and Far Eastern economies began to colonise Europe. Sf had to change to mirror this.

William S Burroughs

Parallel to sf – occasionally published as such – was the writer William S Burroughs (1914-1997), best-known for the novel *The Naked Lunch* (1956). Burroughs was a reformed heroin addict, who began writing whilst he came off junk: comic routines about psychopathic doctors, the link between sex and death, a series of dystopian states, life in the international zone of a north-African town, and various examples of people losing control of their bodies. Throughout Burroughs' work is a Swiftian distrust of the body, or the meat, which is perhaps an influence upon the cyberpunks. After *The Naked Lunch*, Burroughs experimented with cut-ups and fold-ins, ways of randomising texts, giving the whole a dreamlike – or rather nightmarelike – quality.

Burroughs also drew on various genres of pulp fiction: Rider Haggard-esque explorations of jungles, the western, sf (especially in his Venusians) and, most relevant here, the hard-boiled detective genre, with Clem Snide, the Private Asshole. The eponymous *The Wild Boys* (1971) – although they're not limited to that novel – could be viewed as supplying one version of the punk ethos. His work stands as an example of how far things can be pushed in terms of the boundaries of taste; it dealt with drugs, sex, and the end of the body. Most important was Burroughs' ability to coin a phrase, inadvertently providing both bands and other writers with titles.

The Hard-Boiled Detective & Film Noir

Mention of hard-boiled detectives suggests another source: the writings of Dashiell Hammett and Raymond Chandler. Private Investigators are on the edge of society, mixing with the rich and the poor, attempting to right the wrongs in society, but at a cost. On a narrative level, Hammett is probably the more significant, with his sociopath protagonists setting events in motion that they can barely keep track of as they try to play the angles – at times they are as much victims of their actions and the whims of others as they are an influence upon others. The Private Eye begins the novel, and sometimes ends it, not knowing the full story. The incident that started a sequence of events is often forgotten or irrelevant to the action; he will start one job in a town, but finish another.

Chandler's protagonist Philip Marlowe is less of an anti-hero, being a literary descendant of the Arthurian knight. The oft-invoked mean streets are a regular setting in dozens of cyberpunk novels, whether San Francisco, Los Angeles or New York. Chandler brings a poetry to his fiction which is quite distinct from Hammett's more serviceable style; both poles of writing are used by cyberpunks.

The clichés of such fiction recur in cyberpunk: the femme fatale, the wealthy temporary employer, the Mr Big, and the suspicious authorities. The femme fatale is the beautiful woman who may attempt to seduce the hero, and lead him to the brink of disaster. The employer is a morally dubious, but financially successful, person who persuades the protagonist to take on a job, often against the hero's better judgement, and who never quite tells the whole story. The Mr Big is the crime boss, the Godfather, who inevitably contacts the hero at some point to make them an offer they'd better not refuse. And as he goes about his job, skirting criminality, at some point the authorities take an interest, interposing between the hero and his goal.

The look of film noir, from *The Maltese Falcon* (1941) to *The Big Sleep* (1946) and beyond, is also an influence, particular in the cinematic nature of much cyberpunk. Most clearly *Blade Runner* pastiches these films, with its scrolling prologue, rainy city setting, the deadbeat, deadpan delivery of the voice-over from the ex-cop, ex-blade runner Rick Deckard. Kim Newman's *The Night Mayor* (1989) features a virtual reality which is straight out of film noir. Gibson cites the director Howard Hawks – who made *Scarface* (1932), *The Big Sleep* and *The Thing* (1951, uncredited) – as a direct influence.

Cyberpunk: A Provisional Definition

Any definition of cyberpunk has to take both elements of the word into account. Computers have long been part of sf, often as a kind of menace. The power of computers to simulate environments is central to much cyberpunk, with the computer user jacking into this virtual environment or cyberspace by some means: through the spine, through eye sockets, through a chip in the head. The virtual environment liberates the protagonist from the constraints of his or her body, allowing them to take whatever form they choose.

Often some crisis in the real world can be solved by going into the virtual one, a narrative which shares the shape at least of Shakespearean comedies, where the retreat from a city to a green space solves a personal crisis. Other times the entry into the virtual reality is to rescue someone

14

who has got stuck there; this is an even older narrative, echoing Orpheus in the underworld. The critic Joan Gordon rightly noted that the virtual reality represents a dark side to identity or humanity, and is a kind of underworld.

But the computers needn't just be limited to networks; sometimes individuals may be augmented by computers or other equipment – cameras, recording devices, receiving devices. The various types of augmented life – where the flesh is supplemented or replaced by the mechanical – are collectively referred to as the post-human.

The punk is referring to the low life, the working or lower middle-class characters, the have-nots, who populate such fiction. Rather than rocket scientists and beautiful daughters, cyberpunk features drug dealers, drug users, musicians, skateboarders as characters, as well as various hackers. As most writers of cyberpunk are middle-class and (increasingly) middle-aged, some have seen this as nostalgia or wishful thinking on the part of the writers. Some writers, such as Greg Egan, sensibly leave this punk element out of their fiction and concentrate on the possibilities of the virtual (computer- or mathematically-generated environment) or the post-human (augmented thought processes, without quite being the human-machine combination that constitutes the cyborg).

Another aspect of cyberpunk is its linguistic experimentation and stylistic density; the use of computer jargon (real or imagined), street slang or Russian or Japanese loan words is commonplace. For some readers, the brew is just too heady.

Finally the setting must be noted. Aside from computer landscapes, most predominantly the setting is America, as an entirely urbanised environment, with San Francisco and Los Angeles having merged, or a sprawl from Atlanta to Boston. Although a number of recent novels have used eastern-European settings, the cyberpunk world is of the Pacific Rim: Japan, South Africa, Australia, occasionally South America and of course California. There is a mistrust of the Japanese, and behind that a racist fear of an undifferentiated Asian horde. Equally problematic is Gibson's use of voodoo as a parallel to cyberspace.

Post-Cyberpunk & Cyberpunk-Flavoured

There was a sense that cyberpunk was so up to the minute, that by the time the general public noticed cyberpunk, it was all over. Bruce Sterling, in his introduction to *Mirrorshades: The Cyberpunk Anthology* (1986) did much to define and popularise the movement, but he himself wrote things which were not cyberpunk as well. At one point in his introduction Ster-

15

ling argues that cyberpunk is anything written by a cyberpunk author. This is perhaps a homage to Damon Knight who defined sf as that which he pointed at when he said it was sf. Certainly there are stories in *Mirrorshades* which could only be called cyberpunk if we accept this definition and call those writers cyberpunks by default. It is an irony that I will note more than once that much of what I call post-cyberpunk is closer to our idea of cyberpunk than some of the stories collected in the supposedly definitive anthology. A number of the writers who were also in there – in particular Lewis Shiner – produced novels which were only borderline cyberpunk. Rudy Rucker and John Shirley wrote horror as well as sf. Cyberpunk died in about 1986, if not before.

There are further ironies. The central figures of cyberpunk, Gibson and Sterling, turned at the end of the 1980s to writing a steampunk novel, *The Difference Engine* (1990). Steampunk is a sub-genre of sf set in Victorian Britain, part Verne or Wells, part Dickens, predominantly written by US writers and featuring incredible machines, often steam driven, and melodramatic plots featuring grotesque characters and bands of gentlemen. Initially steampunk was a label attached to the writers K W Jeter (especially *Infernal Devices* (1987) and to some extent *Morlock Night* (1979)), Tim Powers (*The Anubis Gates* (1983), although set too early to be called Victorian) and James Blaylock (a number, including *Homunculus* (1986) and *Lord Kelvin's Machine* (1992)), precisely to mark their distinction from writers like Gibson. Gibson's fiction, still sf, still cyberpunk, is now published as general literary fiction.

Cyberpunk novels have continued to be produced, by writers outside the original brotherhood of the anthology. Neal Stephenson and Greg Egan are probably the best-known examples of these writers, and both are discussed in this book. Stephenson is thus a post-cyberpunk, as are many of the British exponents of the sub-genre.

Of course, Britain might be thought to be part of the Old World on which cyberpunk is turning its back; much of cyberpunk is focused on Pacific Rim territories, rather than NATO areas. But just as the Japanese and Chinese culture and economies grew in importance during the 1980s and 1990s, so the European Union, formerly the Common Market, offered a space for the United States of Europe. The fall of the Berlin Wall and the collapse of the USSR equally changed the map of Europe. Some American writers used European settings (Bruce Sterling in *Holy Fire* (1996), for example, William Gibson in *Mona Lisa Overdrive* (1988)), but British writers also responded to the changed political map on their doorstep. Paris and other European locations added an Earth-based exoticism, but

16

the mean streets of cyberpunk could be representative of British inner-city decay, and the brave new world of the information superhighways could form a contrast to the blasted post-industrial landscape of Britain. Just as London could be returned to cobbles and weeds, so there was sometimes a nostalgic memory of an idealised English countryside.

Ken MacLeod's novels (*The Star Fraction* (1995), *The Stone Canal* (1996), *The Cassini Division* (1998) and *The Sky Road* (1999)) combine political musings, space opera, future history and some elements of cyberpunk. Downloaded personalities stored in robots, computer-based civilisations, a secret political conspiracy as a virus and so on were described alongside a Balkanised Britain, a new colony on the other side of a stargate and a future straight out of William Morris' *News From Nowhere* (1890). Given his treatment (and suspicion) of computers and AIs, MacLeod might be viewed as anti-cyberpunk rather than post-cyberpunk. Paul McAuley, aside from a couple of space operas, produced a novel *Fairyland* (1995) and a trilogy, *The Confluence*, which required nanotechnology to work its plot, and hovered on the edge of being fantasy. The European setting of *Fairyland* (1995) is important, as is the setting in Gwyneth Jones' *Kairos* (1988, discussed later).

Just as the cyberpunk movement in the early 1980s looked back to *New Worlds*, so they increasingly looked across to a new British magazine, *Interzone*. Whilst it tried to distance itself from New Wave-style sf, it nevertheless published experimental material more often than writing in the hard sf tradition of, say, Larry Niven or Robert A Heinlein. Alongside new and established British writers, such as Kim Newman, Simon Ings, Brian Stableford and J G Ballard, the magazine published both William Gibson and Bruce Sterling. Sterling even had an opinion column in the magazine for a number of years: ironically many Americans looked to Britain to read material which the British regarded as archetypally American.

With half an eye on *A Clockwork Orange* (both book (1962) and film (1971)), British writers have produced some of the most important post-cyberpunk novels. Jeff Noon, whose *Vurt* (1993) was a cult success of the 1990s, wrote novels which shared a number of tropes of cyberpunk. But with south central Manchester substituting for south central LA, he inevitably tapped into a very English kind of sensibility, and an English rather than American psychedelia. The computers, which are central to much cyberpunk, are almost invisible. I have coined the term 'cyberpunk-flavoured' to describe these and other writings, writings which look like cyberpunk, behave like cyberpunk, are often structured like cyberpunk, but which, nevertheless, *aren't* cyberpunk. I would argue that Greg Egan,

17

whose writing I have noted is hardly punk but very often cyber, is cyber-punk-flavoured.

*

Aside from Pat Cadigan, the cyberpunk movement was predominantly male. Even in post-cyberpunk, there have been much fewer female writers than male. Of course, most of sf in general is written by men. 1970s feminist sf had been concerned with describing utopias or dystopias, and usually required a distant future or alien planet to allow an exploration of the relations between the sexes, rather than the near-future Earth (or near-orbit) setting of much cyberpunk. Nevertheless, the social exploration of such writing was an influence on cyberpunk. Is the leather-skirted, metal-fingernailed Molly featured in William Gibson's early novels one daughter of Alyx? Molly could be seen as a resourceful character able to defend herself. But equally she could be seen as a male fantasy figure, a dominatrix. Whilst some critics accuse cyberpunk (if not all sf) of being toys for the boys, increasing numbers of female writers are producing it, or something like it.

*

As the twenty-first century dawns, as the use of the Internet becomes an everyday reality for a sizeable proportion of the First World population, as every second tv advert is for an Internet Service Provider or some other e-commerce, the original romance of cyberpunk has been lost. Any 20-year-old geek can become an e-millionaire, but the same old big businesses are moving in for the kill. Each new novel is marketed as 'William Gibson meets Quentin Tarantino,' as the tropes become third or fourth hand. But in amidst the trash, the wannabes, the copycats, there is still a core of readable works.

Cyberpunk is dead. Long live the new cyberpunk.

2. Consensual Hallucinations:
The Core Reading

Two writers tower above the cyberpunk movement as its central visionaries: Gibson the breakout writer, and Sterling the polemicist. But between them the cyberpunk movement was shaped and given form – even if others before them had written on similar themes.

William Gibson

William Gibson was born in the USA in 1948, but emigrated to Canada from Virginia after being rejected for the draft to Vietnam. After a period in Toronto, he moved to Vancouver, a city that is part of the Pacific Rim therefore central to cyberpunk's psychic geography. After a number of short stories later collected in *Burning Chrome* (1986) – including 'Johnny Mnemonic,' a story quite different from the film, and the breakthrough to the alternate world 'The Gernsback Continuum' – Gibson's vision of the future was given flight in the novel *Neuromancer*, which won the Hugo, Nebula and Philip K Dick Awards. Despite the high-tech world he depicts, Gibson had had very little personal contact with computers; *Neuromancer* was written on a manual typewriter prior to the home computer revolution of the 1980s. If only because he is deluged with faxes everyday, he has refused for many years to have an e-mail address, and was reluctant about trying out the worldwide web; perhaps his imagination might be compromised by being confronted by the reality of what he had imagined.

As each new novel is published, so Gibson's readership seems to increase, and his last three novels have been published as mainstream rather than sf. Nevertheless, his reputation does still largely rest on *Neuromancer*, which is probably the sf novel that has been written about by academics more than any other. Gibson was one of the many authors to write a script for the third *Alien* film (which has been pirated on-line), and he also wrote the script for *Johnny Mnemonic*. The screenplay has been published as a separate volume.

Neuromancer (1984)

The Set-Up: Case is a console cowboy, who has stolen from his employers and has been punished by having his nervous system filled with a mycotoxin that prevents him from jacking into the matrix. Armitage cures and then blackmails him into stealing data – the personality of Dixie Flatliner, in read-only memory form – and to carry out his plan. Behind

Armitage is Wintermute, an Artificial Intelligence, who sees the bigger picture of what's going on in cyberspace... and who is out there...

The Hero: Case is the master hacker, able to send his personality into the computer networks. Hanging over him is the threat of poison from within: mycotoxin sacs sewn into his arteries, slowly dissolving. The body just can't be trusted, nor can other people, and he longs to leave his meat behind, unlike Dixie Flatliner, who longs to be erased.

The Femme Fatale: Molly, with her black leather trousers, mirrored contact lenses and retractable, steel, fingernails is the stuff of fetishes, and is not so much the object of desire (although a version of her is in a cabaret hologram) as the active sexual partner. Liberated woman or wet dream?

Playing The Angles: For all his proficiency, Case never quite knows what's going on, whether it's who he is really working for, what he is really trying to achieve or what is really going on. Like hundreds of private eyes before him, a book of matches guides him to where he ought to go, and a phone call from the Mr Big – here Wintermute – makes him an offer he shouldn't really refuse, and would help him learn something to his advantage.

The Style: From the famous opening line 'The sky above the port was the color of television, tuned to a dead channel,' it is clear that this is going to be a stylish book. Some of Gibson's computer jargon is real, some has since been adopted. For some the surface shine of *Neuromancer* has proved too information dense, but Gibson is clearly a master stylist. Through the early chapters Case is described again and again in mechanical terms, as if he is a machine rather than a human being. The other chain of symbolism is that of eyes, watching and looking, a symbolism which curiously coincides with *Blade Runner* (1982).

The Underworld: To know the name of an AI is to control them, perhaps, or at least that's how it works with demons. The AI Neuromancer's name works on a number of levels: the neuro being a reference to the nervous system, the new romancer referring to the romance of the new, especially technology, and the whole being a letter away from Necromancer, the summoner of the dead. And under his power, Case does meet up with his dead girlfriend.

The Pay-Off: The key starting point for reading cyberpunk, a book whose moment can never quite be recaptured.

Count Zero (1986)

The Set-Up: Turner has been assassinated and is rebuilt to help bring in Mitchell, who has been working for Maas Biolabs. Bobby, aka Count Zero, is lucky to survive a bad experience in the matrix. He goes in search of more powerful software. Marly is employed to locate a number of artworks for a boss whose cancer-riddled body is in a vat. Naturally, there is a connection...

The Hero: Turner is the more experienced, resourceful hero, able to smell a trap in advance. Count Zero, for all his bravado, is much more at the mercy of others.

The Femme Fatale: Marly is tough, but not tough enough. Angie Mitchell, who does defect, has sex with Turner in that post-James Bond rescue kind of way.

Playing The Angles: The three narratives take it more or less in turns to be told, and it is not until very late that they come together, rather unsatisfactorily. They are all set in the same world though, the world of the Atlanta-Boston Sprawl and the matrix. The action is again international – India, Mexico, Paris, New York and even into space. Virek, the novel's Mr Big, is able to keep tabs on his charge despite being on ice, and everybody seems to be bugging, or being bugged by, everybody else. Just as well that you can tell your flying machine to lie about where it's been.

The Style: Computer terminology jostles with hints at Haitian culture and voodoo, whilst the opening pays homage to Robert Johnson.

The Underworld: Turner and Count Zero are in a sense the undead, having been repaired after death-like experiences. And some of the characters discuss cyberspace in terms of voodoo.

The Pay-Off: Neither Turner's nor Marly's missions seem enough in themselves to sustain a novel, and the Count's actions seem obscure. It lacks the sharpness of *Neuromancer*. 'Barrytown', a recurring setting in the novel, takes its name from a Steeley Dan track, as did Roddy Doyle for his comic trilogy of *The Commitments*, *The Snapper* and *The Van*. 'The sky above the Liffey was the color of Guinness...'

Mona Lisa Overdrive (1988)

The Set-Up: Seven years later. Kumiko, daughter of a powerful Japanese, is sent to London after the death of her mother. Slick Henry, in Dog Solitude, is hired to look after a body of a man in cyberspace. In Malibu Angie, fresh out of detox, wonders where Bobby is. And a prostitute named Mona has been chosen for her likeness to Angie to take part in some kind of kidnapping.

The Hero: None of the male characters are particularly active and heroic – Bobby is in cyberspace, Slick keeps on having fugues, his friend Gentry is too petty and strung out and Colin, Kumiko's virtual guide to London, can only stand and watch.

The Femme Fatale: On the other hand, Angie still holds a few surprises, Kumiko can take remarkable care of herself for a 13-year-old in a strange country, and her friend Sally, also involved in the kidnapping plot, is none other than Molly.

Playing The Angles: All roads lead to Bobby, aka Count Zero, who seems to have dropped from sight for seven years. Quite why they want him is anyone's guess, but it's all tied up with the nature of cyberspace, and the sense that it all changed 14 years ago, when Case was last spotted.

The Style: Fast moving, but to little effect; the four parallel threads that later come together mean than it's quite hard to follow the action, and each slice of the narrative is very slim. Gibson varies the rhythm by not having the four occur in the same order each time, but that throws off the pattern rather than prevent monotony.

The Pay-Off: This is meant to be stand alone, but there would be little point in coming to it without having read at least one of the earlier novels. A slightly different light is cast on these events, but there's a tying-up of threads rather than anything significantly new. Oh, and Kumiko is surely an earlier version of Chia McKenzie from *Idoru*.

Virtual Light (1993)

The Set-Up: San Francisco, 2005. Berry Rydell is an ex-cop, and now works for a private security agency. He is assigned to track down some stolen goods, except that the owner of them has been murdered and had his tongue cut out. Meanwhile Chevette, the thief, is unaware of the danger she has brought upon herself.

The Hero: Rydell has had a chequered career, and has almost been the subject of the true story television programme *Cops In Trouble*. He is an efficient investigator, certainly more so than the cops he bumps into, although they might not be on the level anyway. Certainly there is the sense that Rydell doesn't quite know what's going on.

The Femme Fatale: Chevette comes originally from Oregon, but now makes her living as a bicycle courier. She scams her way into a party and takes the dark glasses, unaware of what they are.

Playing The Angles: The glasses project data into the perception system of whoever wears them, and the data that these store is about the future of San Francisco. This is (ahem) virtually the only appearance of cybernetic technology in the whole novel. Instead the novel is dominated by the mean streets of the big city, gunplay, corrupt cops, narrow escapes and reality tv. There is even a cult that depends upon the continual watching of television – with the film *Videodrome* seen as being the work of the devil.

The Style: The narratives of Rydell and Chevette more or less alternate until they meet halfway through the novel, Rydell's story being written in the past tense, Chevette's in the present. There is also the narrative of Yamazaki, which serves mostly to fill in the background of this near-future world.

The Pay-Off: Arguably cyberpunk lite, although there are many tiny telling details of a tightly extrapolated near future. The glasses are, however, little more than a MacGuffin to set the twin narratives going.

Idoru (1996)

The Set-Up: Colin Laney, who is able to piece information together about people from the data trail they leave behind them, is employed to investigate the music star Rez by the gangster-like minder, Blackwell. Blackwell fears that someone has got through his security net to Rez, and fears it might be linked to Rez's announcement that he is to wed Rei Toei, an idoru or virtual media star. Meanwhile the 14-year-old Chia McKenzie, of the Seattle chapter of the Rez fan club, travels to Japan to see if the rumour of the affair between Rez and Rei is true.

The Hero: Colin's abilities were the result of experimentation with drugs, with him as an unwitting guinea pig. He had worked for Slitscan, a television network, exposing the private lives of celebrities. However one such investigation led to the suicide of the daughter of one of his subjects, and he left the company. This new job was obtained for him through the efforts of Berry Rydell, now a hotel security guard, and Yamazaki, revealed as a student of popular culture.

The Femme Fatale: In some ways the seductive Rei Toei, the entirely virtual star of Japan. Kathy Torrance, Colin's former boss and lover, is also there to make trouble for him.

Playing The Angles: There's a sense of computer paranoia here, that the information we've accessed can reveal things about ourselves that we don't want others to know. After all, they reckon they can deduce things about our personalities and income from the contents of our shopping trolleys (hmm, bread, bagels, pizza and hommous, all reduced to clear... not sure I want that revealed about me). Equally there is a narrative of the behaviour of fans – something in the tradition of Beatlemania, or the more recent teenage girl desires for Take That, Boyzone, or whatever the current popular beat combo is. Chia, to complicate matters, has carried someone else's suitcase through customs, and ended up with an object that she could well do without.

The Style: Another ping-pong narrative, alternating between Chia and Colin, although Colin's tale is complicated by his memories/retelling of his earlier career. The two threads do overlap, but are mostly separate.

The Pay-Off: This feels like a middle book in a trilogy (which it is, of course) – nothing is actually resolved, the problems seem as deep as ever, the puzzle of how you can marry a computer-constructed hologram seems unanswered and so on. But it's above all a thriller, and a very readable novel with a fascinating image of a Tokyo rebuilt after an earthquake and a virtual version of Venice.

All Tomorrow's Parties (1999)

The Set-Up: Laney can perceive in the data flow of the world that a massive change is coming, like the change that happened in 1911 (don't ask – Laney doesn't know either). He also perceives that tycoon Cody Levine is not only connected to the change, but is doing everything he can to bring it about. Unfortunately Laney has fallen ill and now has stalker syndrome, a result of the drug given him as a child to enable him to perceive data traces. So he employs Berry Rydell to start investigating events in San Francisco, although he can't say precisely what Rydell is doing.

The Hero: Laney is more or less static throughout the novel, speaking to Rydell through telephones or virtual light spectacles, arranging for packages to be delivered, and so on. Rydell is again the competent investigator out of his depth, which is hardly unexpected when people aren't telling him the full story of what's going on. His rôle in the mean time is often to be beaten up, knocked out or threatened with death. And he still hasn't had his chance to appear on *Cops In Trouble*.

The Femme Fatale: Chevette is back, perhaps really regretting that she split up with Rydell, but still remembering that they had little in common when the action stopped. She doesn't have a lot to do until coincidence ensures her reunion with Rydell in a nightclub. Rei Toei is also back, having developed as a personality and left behind Rez as an infantile male (is there a critique of cyberpunk characters in there?)

Playing The Angles: Chaos theory and prediction seem to be the core here: how can you predict the future from the mass of data that the world

24

generates? Laney can clearly ride the data, although it may kill him, as can Cody. For Rydell, with the tools and devices put at his disposal, and the right people turning up at the right time, the future seems mapped out. Although he, of course, can't see it.

The Style: Rydell's is the primary narrative, more or less alternating with the lives of a considerable cast of other characters: Maryalice, Yamazaki, Laney, Chevette and so on, across seventy short chapters, many less than a page long. The thirty-second attention span is rewarded here.

The Underworld: Well, the title's a *Velvet Underground* track, off *The Velvet Underground And Nico* album (you know, the one with the banana on the cover).

The Pay-Off: The ending, as you'd expect is ambiguous, and as for the change, well, presumably it has happened. Still, the future San Francisco is fascinating, as is the return to the community in the abandoned Oakland Bay Bridge, a setting first used in *Virtual Light*, and also used (albeit with a different bridge) in *Johnny Mnemonic*.

In 1992, Gibson published *Agrippa: (A Book Of The Dead)*, a text that was only available on a floppy disk and which was designed to be read once before it erased itself. Naturally this presented a challenge to hackers all over the world, and, naturally, the text was hacked and can be found on-line (for example at http://www.dcs.gla.ac.uk/SF-Archives/Misc/Agrippa). It is an account of old photographs, relating to Gibson's father, a reference to the draft, and how Gibson knew he was a writer. *Agrippa* is a poem, in free verse, with some striking imagery, but at times it struggles to rise above the level of an annotated list (which is perhaps a rich thing to say in a book like this one...).

Bruce Sterling

Sterling was born in 1954 and had his first story published in an anthology of Texan sf, *Lone Star Universe* (1976). His first novel, set on a ship which sails across the fine sand of an alien planet, was *Involution Ocean* (1978). Whilst his second novel wasn't cyberpunk, it had some elements which would later be typical of the genre.

Although he has only produced two or three volumes that could be considered cyberpunk (and both of these are on a far more cosmic scale than the more down-to-Earth (or down-to-near-Earth orbit) than Gibson's writings), he is a pivotal figure in the field. In the pseudonymously-edited fanzine *Cheap Truth* published in the mid-1980s, Sterling attacked much of the other sf of the field and began to set out his manifesto for a new kind of writing. In 1986 he published the collection *Mirrorshades*, which drew together a group of writers which he perceived to be part of a cyberpunk generation, and wrote a polemical introduction where he defined the writing as information dense, embracing rather than afraid of technology, embodying a do-it-yourself, punk ethos and so on. If a number of the stories in there don't now appear to be cyberpunk, Sterling prepared the ground for us by saying that cyberpunk fiction was anything written by a cyberpunk writer. At the same time, the cutting edge, avant-garde nature of the sub-genre has led many critics to suggest that the anthology was the death knell of cyberpunk, having pinned it down as a literary movement.

The Artificial Kid (1980)

The Set-Up: On the planet Reverie, the professional combat artist R T goes on the run from the ruling Cabal with Saint Anne Twiceborn and Moses Moses, a man who has awoken from a sleep of several centuries.

The Hero: R T, the eponymous Artificial Kid, is actually Rominauld Tanglin, once one of the leaders of the planet, who had a version of his personality inserted into a body before his death. The Kid is ultraviolent, but is medically fixed at a point prior to puberty, and goes everywhere with cameras filming his actions.

The Femme Fatale: Saint Anne Twiceborn was born into a Church on the planet Niwilind, but has a sexual past of significance to the novel. Having fought for the preservation of moas, she is now a political refugee.

Playing The Angles: Behind the punk attitude of the Artificial Kid, lies a political thriller of sorts, as the politics of the past collide with the science of the present. This is, however, just an excuse for a series of adventures as he goes on the run.

The Underworld: Moses Moses, the Artificial Kid/Rominauld Tanglin and his creator, Professor Crowbar, all in some way attempt to cheat death with success at least on the genetic or personality level.

The Style: The Kid says at one point that style is a weapon; this is quite a talky book though, as the characters tell their stories to each other. These are nested within the Kid's overall first-person narration.

The Pay-Off: Most of the novel is set on a floating island; and having echoed *Moby Dick* in *Involution Ocean*, here refers to *Pinocchio*. Fun but fairly forgettable.

Crystal Express (1989)

The stories in the first section of this collection are all set in the Mechanist/Shapers universe, and predate *Schismatrix* in publication: 'Swarm' (*Fantasy and Science Fiction*, April 1982), 'Spider Rose' (*Fantasy and Science Fiction*, August 1982), 'Cicada Queen' (*Universe* 13, edited by Terry Carr, New York: Doubleday, 1983), 'Sunken Gardens' (Omni, June 1984) and 'Life in the Mechanist/Shaper Era: 20 Evocations' (*Interzone* 7, 1984). The Shapers are one form of post-human, who are the product of genetic engineering, and are sometimes known as the Reshapers. The other form of post-human are the Mechanists, who are humans with artificial body parts, whether additional parts of the brain or prosthetic limbs. Having more or less left Earth behind, the two races interact with each other as rivals and with various alien races. It is perhaps easiest to start with the final story of the sequence, which explains some of the background, although 'story' is perhaps not quite the right word – the pieces are incidents in the universe Sterling has imagined.

'Swarm' documents the encounter of a Shaper, Captain-Doctor Simon Afriel with an alien hive mind, and his wager that somehow humanity (or rather post-humanity) will survive when so many other species with space colonies have died out. 'Spider Rose' records the encounter of a 200-year-old Mechanist in the region of Uranus with a race of trading aliens, and their gift of a genetically-engineered pet to her. In 'Cicada Queen' the induction of Landau into Poly Carbon clique is described, and then his exile as a different kind of post-human. This story is particularly dense in information and ideas, with a complex exploration of the politics of Sterling's imagined universe. 'Sunken Gardens' features the terraforming of Mars, a planet inhabited by Mechanists and Shapers.

Schismatrix (1985)

The Set-Up: Abelard Lindsay is exiled from the Mare Tranquillitatis People's Circumlunar Zaibatsu, and his old friend and rival Constantine. Over the next century he moves through a series of locations and political affiliations, sometimes trying a scam, sometimes simply trying to fit in.

The Hero: Lindsay had been an ambassador with Constantine between his people and the Shapers, and they had been discredited when the Mechanists began to dominate the politics of the post-human solar system. Out on his own, he is always trying to make new alliances; he is resourceful and has a conjuring tongue and (less metaphorically) an artificial arm.

Playing The Angles: This novel needs to be read alongside the stories in *Crystal Express*, as both cast a light on each other: Simon Afriel from 'Swarm', the Cicada Queen, terraforming planets and so forth. Lindsay, in his various guises, is the one constant in an otherwise fast-moving, system-spanning novel.

The Style: The very pace is its potential downfall: it can be too information-dense, with political systems and neologisms taken as read before the action shifts five years or fifty. The novel is thus episodic, ever picaresque, and just when you think you've got a handle on things, the location shifts. And characters reoccur from earlier in the narrative, sometimes in disguise, sometimes as computer simulations. Many novelists would get a whole novel out of what Sterling tosses out (or away) in a single paragraph.

The Pay-Off: This is a very different cyberpunk to Gibson's – for a start the computers are virtually non-existent, Earth is off-stage for much of the action and it's set centuries not months into the future. The punk attitude is there though, and it explores the post-human existence that comes out of cyberpunk's obsession with the human-machine interface. Cyberpunk would be very different if this, not *Neuromancer*, had won all the awards.

The Shaper/Mechanist short stories and the novel *Schismatrix* are also available in a single volume, *Schismatrix Plus* (1996).

Not all the stories in *Crystal Express* are in the Mechanist/Shapers sequence, and other non-sequence stories appear in the collection *Globalhead* (1992). *Heavy Weather* (1994) is a novel set in a world of massive storms caused by ecological meltdown. More recently he has written the Arthur C Clarke Award-Winning *Distraction* (1999), an account of a near-future America on the brink of collapse, and the exploits of a spin doctor trying to hold onto power and keep one step ahead of social chaos. Personally I'd find the satire more convincing if Neal Stephenson and J Frederick George, writing as Stephen Bury, hadn't done it much better in their fictional account of the presidential campaign of 1996, *Interface* (1994). Sterling has also produced non-fiction, most substantially *The Hacker Crackdown: Law And Disorder On The Electronic Frontier* (1992), a book inspired by the raid on TSR Games in Switzerland and the removal of their computers, and moving into a wider investigation of computer crime.

3. The Cyberpunk Movement

Whilst William Gibson and Bruce Sterling are the more famous writers of cyberpunk, and probably the most successful, they were not alone. Bruce Sterling gathered a number of such writers together for an anthology, *Mirrorshades*, and introduced it with a polemical account of the sub-genre. Nevertheless, the writers were gathered together in what Bruce Sterling saw as a mood of sf, in the tradition of Delany, Bester, Dick, Burroughs and so on, offering a new counter-culture (one which embraced technology unlike the generation of the 1960s), a global culture of remix and interferences, interzones, interminglings, a new vision of sf and of the world. Few, if any, of the writers set out to write cyberpunk consciously, some – such as Greg Bear – would even reject the label. Many of the writers also wrote or went on to write horror, fantasy, non-fiction or magic realism; Greg Bear in particular has produced genre sf rather than cyberpunk, although some recent novels at least nod in the direction of AIs and the near future.

It is ironic that many of the writers included in the anthology, indeed many of the pieces included in it, are less comfortably cyberpunk than some of the material I am going to discuss in the chapters on post-cyberpunk and cyberpunk-flavoured fiction. This chapter discusses the writers who were published in *Mirrorshades*.

Greg Bear

Gregory Dale Bear would no doubt deny that he is a cyberpunk writer, and the story he has in *Mirrorshades*, 'Petra', hardly seems to disprove any such assertion. The tale of a repressive world within an enormous cathedral after the death of God, the flavour is closer to Mervyn Peake than William Gibson. There are hints that some of the non-human characters are mechanical – a power supply of one of them seems to be running down – but it doesn't seem very close to the sub-genre identified with the anthology. (It is, however, a delightful story).

Born in 1951, Bear was first published in 1967, and many of his novels feature complex characters against a hard science background; in the case of *Blood Music*, genetic engineering and viruses. Further novels have been on a more cosmological scale, although the near-future worlds of *Queen Of Angels* (1990) and / (aka *Slant* (1997)) are of interest.

Blood Music (1985)

The Set-Up: Virgil Ulam is conducting his own experiments on genetically-modified cells using the facilities at the company he is working for. When his boss fires him, he smuggles the new cells out of the laboratory in his own bloodstream. At first he seems healthier than he has ever been, but then he begins to transform into a new type of human, and the cells within him are behaving like a virus, infecting others.

The Hero: Given the structure of the novel, it's difficult to isolate one figure as a hero from the ensemble of characters. The scientist who starts the virus is misguided rather than mad. His boss could be seen as standing in the way of progress, but it is probably just as well he did. Michael Bernard and Edward Milligan do their best to understand the cellular matter and prevent its spread, but even they aren't quite heroes. The characters are reasonably well developed for cyberpunk.

Playing The Angles: The genetically-engineered cellular matter seems to take on an identity of its own, a kind of collective group identity within the individual host. The host is in part a god to it, but they also invite the god to join them and become one of them. Late on in the narrative we have an account of such a joining, after seeing some characters reject it; we can, just, glimpse a next stage of evolution. And this being hard science fiction, there is also a sub-theme of the Uncertainty Principle, and the impact observation – in this case by trillions of observers – has on the universe. Coo.

The Style: There are moments of technical stuff, and voices from within (the DNA talking), but basically this is constructed as an episodic, realist novel.

The Underworld: A long shot this, but Virgil (aka Vergil) was Dante's guide in the underworld of *The Divine Comedy.*

The Pay-Off: A very fruitful novel – the ethics of the international world, of genetic engineering and an exploration of the nature of the virus as invader – the invader from within. Beyond Vergil's do-it-yourself attitude to experimentation, you'd be hard-pressed to identify a punk ethos though.

Pat Cadigan

Pat Cadigan was born in 1953 in the United States, but in the 1990s moved to London where she married the critic Christopher Fowler. Her first fiction appeared in *Shayol*, a magazine she edited. Further short fiction has been collected in *Patterns* (1989), *Home By The Sea* (1992) and

Dirty Work (1993). Her first novel, *Mindplayers*, and third, *Fools*, both won the Arthur C Clarke Award, the first time the same writer has won it twice. She is the only female writer to be associated with the first generation of cyberpunk writers, indeed she has been hailed as the 'Queen of Cyberpunk.' There is perhaps a problem in much cyberpunk that it depicts female characters as femmes fatales, and thus either as empowering or degrading figures or a misogynistic depiction. Given Gibson's move into the mainstream, Sterling's parallel non-cyberpunk work, and the broad shift out of the movement by other authors in *Mirrorshades* (or failure to produce the second novel) Cadigan is the author who has explored cyberpunk most consistently; she is certainly one of the most interesting figures.

Mindplayers (1987)

The Set-Up: Allie Haas has been arrested for illegal use of mindplaying equipment and is offered the chance to be a pathosfinder – part-cyberspace guide, part psychiatrist.

The Hero: Deadpan Allie is clearly the main character, although she is not superheroic: she can make mistakes, she doesn't know all the answers and she suspects her personality isn't just her own.

The Femme Fatale: Jerry Wirerammer, the (male) friend who got her arrested in the first place, crops up from time to time to tempt her into his world of bootleg dreams and memories; after a while it's unclear as to whether he is Jerry or a cloned copy of a bootleg of Jerry...

Playing The Angles: We follow Allie's career as she guides mindplayers, counsels those who have split up from others who mindplayed with them, or tries to retrieve the minds of the recently deceased.

The Style: The novel is episodic, as we follow her on each assignment. The sub-plot of Jerry Wirerammer forms a kind of continuity.

The Underworld: When Allie is assigned to retrieve the confused mind of a dead person we seem to go beyond the realm of the living; forever afterwards she is not convinced that her mind is clean.

The Pay-Off: An impressive debut, demonstrating a world where cyberspace is at work and making money for people (something which Cadigan develops with the concept of billable time in *Tea From An Empty Cup*).

Synners (1991)

The Set-Up: The Synners are a group of video makers and hackers, creators of simulations, who are hot-wired into the net in a throat-cutting corporate future. A new intelligence, Dr Artie Fish, is alive in the net and it has contacted them. And not a moment too soon, as they're going to need all the allies they can get: there is a virus loose that could take out all the computers, and the console jockeys riding them.

The Heroes: This is an ensemble piece, with a large cast of characters. Sam is the leading female, and Mark the most important male, but much of the novel is the individuals doing what they do best. Whilst the apocalypse creeps up behind them...

Playing The Angles: Cadigan's early novels are everyday life in cyberspace, and there in a sense that there's a price to pay for access to it – the Synners are free-market economists or entrepreneurs in their own small way. This financial aspect is perhaps forgotten as the narrative – such as it is – progresses.

The Style: This novel falls into the trap of not quite making the real/virtual worlds distinct enough for my taste – but perhaps when you wire in so often there is no distinction.

The Underworld: Jones commits suicide frequently for kicks.

The Pay-Off: Cadigan's longest novel, and the least sharp. By the time of *Tea From An Empty Cup* she can make her point in two hundred pages, but this novel feels flabby.

Fools (1992)

The Set-Up: Marva, a method actress, finds herself in a club called Davy Jones' Locker, with more money than she ought to have, and the memory of killing a cop. Another woman, Marceline, also remembers killing a cop. And then there's Marya, a Brain Cop, who's undercover. I think.

The Hero: Again female characters are to the fore... Marva, Marceline and Marya. I think.

Playing The Angles: Is Marva truly herself or is she still stuck in a rôle? Has she melded personalities with Marceline by escorting her, possibly in cyberspace? And then there's the undercover cop who might be one of them, or they all may be a character suffering from multiple personality disorder. I think.

The Style: The three different voices are distinguished by three different typefaces, which at last allows some semblance of beginning to make sense of it all.

The Underworld: Davy Jones' Locker sounds pretty bleeding subterranean to me.

The Pay-Off: An ambitious novel that is perhaps too ambitious in its exploration of the melding of personalities and the implications of acting and avatars in cyberspace. It's supposedly set in the same universe as *Mindplayers*, but the only real indication of this is a mention of Jerry Wirerammer. One to read and reread, or just to batten down the hatches and enjoy. I think.

Tea From An Empty Cup (1998)

The Set-Up: A boy's body has been found in a cubicle in a near future equivalent of the cybercafé or games arcade, and Lieutenant Konstantin is drafted in to investigate how someone could die in the virtual world (AR, for *Artificial* Reality) and real life (RL). The boy is called both Shantih Love and Tomoyuki Iguchi, but neither of those appear to be real names, and his true identity is lost or irrelevant. Konstantin, a novice at AR, attempts to retrace Shantih's virtual steps, and goes in search of Body Sativa, whom she believes can help her solve this and half a dozen other AR/RL murders.

The Style: A ping-pong narrative structure; after a conversational first chapter, the narrative alternates between the story of Yuki (headed 'Empty Cup') and Konstantin ('Death in the Promised Land'). Yuki is in search of her friend Tomoyuki Iguchi, who has gone missing, and like Konstantin goes looking for him wearing a version of the Tomoyuki body. Whereas the Konstantin thread is police procedural, Yuki's is much more philosophical, posing questions about the nature of identity, and perhaps demonstrates just how far an author can go in metaphysical terms.

The Underworld: The Underworld here is both AR and the lost Japan, which may be resurrected in RL or be another virtual theme park. Konstantin and, to a much greater thematic extent, Yuki both find themselves in the Orpheus rôle.

Playing The Angles: To say too much would be to risk revealing the climax of the novel, but reading through you discover that virtually every identity presented by a character is simply a persona obscuring another identity. Yuki's apotheosis offers another such scenario, and answers a nagging question at the back of my mind: we've seen at least three versions of Tomoyuki on-line, but I don't think we're told about his real-life body. In the final paragraph of the novel, I believe this conundrum is solved. Her latest novel, *Dervish Is Digital* (2000) is a sequel to *Tea From An Empty Cup*.

Marc Laidlaw

Laidlaw was born in 1960, and his story '400 Boys' appeared in *Mirrorshades*. His first novel is of interest to us here, but it is quite subtly cyberpunk. His subsequent novels, *Neon Lotus* (1988), *Kalifornia* (1993) and *The Orchid Eater* (1994), are satires or non-sf.

Dad's Nuke (1985)

The Set-Up: Dad is the head of the Johnson family in an idyllic enclave of suburban America after the collapse. He's locked into an arms race with his neighbour, the Smiths, and faces a change in his situation as three children have hit puberty.

The Hero: Dad is a character out of a sitcom, wanting to keep up with the neighbours, wanting to join the local men's club, and failing to quite keep his family in control.

Playing The Angles: His eldest son, Virgil, is getting married, he has just told his second son, P J that he (P J) is homosexual, and his eldest daughter is about to have treatment to make her undergo puberty (which will hopefully ensure that she gives up her love for his neighbours' son). But thankfully there is hope with the youngest child, who has been genetically-engineered to digest radioactive waste. All of the children have been engineered to make a balanced family, and ageing is controlled by drugs.

The Style: Clearly comic, with an awful lot of inventive details, and hints of satire on the arms race, the image of the home as castle, religious movements, and small town/suburban life in America. Each family has a one-hour programme about their day on the cable tv, anticipating docusoaps by a good ten years.

The Underworld: The family go on a disastrous virtual trip to Yosemite, and get trapped in there by a computer failure. The idyll seems to be turning into hell.

The Pay-Off: On the surface inoffensive and good fun, but a darker side is subtly obscured.

Tom Maddox

Daniel Thomas Maddox, born 1945, is a professor of languages and literature and began publishing fiction in 1985. His story in *Mirrorshades* is called 'Snake Eyes' and may be set in the same universe as *Halo*; it's the tale of someone coming to terms with a brain implant and control by an AI, Aleph. Most of Maddox's short fiction appeared in *Omni*, and *Halo* is his only published novel to date.

Halo (1991)

The Set-Up: Mikhail Gonzales, having narrowly avoided being killed by an ICBM in an aeroplane, is sent to the space habitat Halo to observe an experiment: Jerry Chapman is dying and they are trying to store his identity whilst he undergoes surgery. The surgeon brought in for the operation is Diane Heywood, former lover of Chapman. And when the process goes wrong, the AI which runs Halo, Aleph, begins to sulk.

The Hero: Gonzales is clearly removed from the action, being an observer rather than one of the two lovers. He has a multicultural background – Russian Jew, Hispanic, black, Cuban – but this seems to add little.

Playing The Angles: In the epigraphs to the chapters quotations are taken from theorists Jean Baudrillard – who discusses the way that reality itself is turning into a simulation of itself – and Donna Haraway – whose essay 'A Manifesto For Cyborgs' did much to introduce cybertheory to feminism and ended with the preference for women being cyborgs rather than goddesses. An opposite opinion is mentioned in passing in the novel. Meanwhile it is clear that the Western economy is being propped up by the East, with famous American brand names spliced with Japanese and Korean ones. This is building a background world, rather than significant.

The Style: The novel is straightforwardly written, in the third person, with occasional interventions from Aleph itself.

The Underworld: Twins appear towards the end of the novel: Alice and Eurydice, complete with reference to Orpheus. Later on there is an echo of Persephone's split life between the underworld and the everyday world.

The Pay-Off: The hotshot international opening seems rather at odds with the philosophical explorations of the rest of the book. The first part punk, the rest cyber.

Rudy Rucker

Rudolf von Bitter Rucker was born in 1946, and has a background in mathematics. In fact he might be considered more in the line of such nineteenth-century mathematician fantasists as Charles H Hinton, Lewis Carroll and Edwin Abbott than cyberpunk. His first novel to be published in book form, *White Light, Or What Is Cantor's Continuum Problem?* (1980), features a mathematician, Felix Rayman, who enters a realm, Cimön, inhabited by his heroes in the field, Cantor, Hilbert and Einstein. As he climbs Mount On in search of absolute infinity, he experiences or explains a number of aspects of infinity. Cimön is in some senses an underworld, featuring the dead, transmigrated individuals (a reference to Kafka's *Metamorphosis*) and Jesus and Satan; it is difficult to be absolutely (ahem) certain whether the realm is real or imaginary, which surely is the point.

His story in *Mirrorshades*, 'Tales Of Houdini,' is an account of the escapes of Harry Houdini. He has gone on to write more short stories (some with Marc Laidlaw), poetry, a steampunk and several cyberpunk novels, non-fiction on mathematics and computer software. With Robert Anton Wilson and Peter Lamborn, he edited the experimental cyberpunk anthology, *Semiotext(e) SF* (1988). Aside from his four Ware novels, his collection of short stories, poetry and non-fiction *Transreal!* (1991) is worth seeking out.

Software (1982)

The Set-Up: Cobb Anderson was the designer of the artificial intelligences which run the robots. When they revolt, setting up a colony on the Moon, Anderson is accused of treason. Now an old man with a failing body, Anderson is offered the chance to be preserved as a robot.

The Hero: Anderson's age means that he is confused when he sees a double of himself, and no one pays particular attention to him if he says something odd is going on. Nevertheless when he is on form, he is still able to think philosophically.

Playing The Angles: There is a second double, of Sta-Hi Mooney, the son of the policeman who lives next to Mooney. Sta-Hi is a waste of space, dropping acid at any opportunity, whereas his replacement is well behaved and gets a better job. Which version is better, the slacker or the drone?

The Style: The style is reminiscent of Philip K Dick – robots smuggled to Earth in packing crates, an ambiguous patriarch, the policeman who lives next door and has to do his job somehow, made awkward by his son, and the leader of the robot revolution, Ralph Numbers, who may or may not be a good, er, person. The robots have rebelled against rule by Isaac Asimov's three laws of robotics, which puts humanity's benefit ahead of robot health.

The Pay-Off: A fun novel which poses some questions about identity, and continuity of identity in a new body. It won the Philip K Dick Award.

Wetware (1988)

The Set-Up: 2030: Sta-Hi Mooney, now a private investigator calling himself Stahn, is hired to track down Della. Meanwhile Cobb Anderson, killed ten years ago by Sta-Hi, has been resurrected in a new body: wetware.

The Hero: Stahn disappears for huge swathes of the action, but he had a wife named Wendy who has been killed and who may now be resurrected if he plays his cards right. And he still hasn't kicked the drugs habit. Cobb doesn't get to do much to be honest.

The Femme Fatale: Della, who is pregnant, and Berenice, a robot who learned to speak by reading Edgar Allan Poe's prose.

Playing The Angles: Humans begat the robots or Boppers, and Boppers try to build themselves a new body every ten months or so, but now they are able to merge their software with the wetware of DNA and produce a meat robot, Manchile.

The Style: Each chapter is given a specific date – either in November or December 2030, or in 2031 – and so the narrative doesn't have to unfold in strict chronological order. Fortunately this is an aberration which stops after the first half dozen or so chapters. Again there are echoes of Philip K Dick.

The Underworld: Anderson has come back from the dead, and imagines talking to God, who describes himself as Eurydice to Anderson's Orpheus. Wendy is also brought back from the dead, and it might be that the name is an act of homage somewhere along the line to the character in J M Barrie's *Peter Pan* (1904), who said that death would be an awfully big adventure.

The Pay-Off: Not as satisfying as the first novel in the Ware sequence, but still inventive, echoing bits of Philip K Dick (drug use, an encounter with god, a character named Charles Freck (compare *A Scanner Darkly*) and so on); the novel is even dedicated to Dick.

Freeware (1997)

The Set-Up: The 2050s. Moldies are an artificial life form made from a soft, malleable plastic and genetically-engineered fungi, molds and algae. Like the robots before them, they are not universally liked, and there is a Heritagist movement against them, in favour of pure humanity. Randy Karl Tucker, the illegitimate great-grandson of Cobb Anderson, uses Moldies for sex, and begins working on the manufacture of devices which can control Moldies for a company in India - he is blackmailed into leaking the secrets of the process. Meanwhile Tre Dietz has been happily working on all sorts of software, and the mold-based limpware, until the day his wife is kidnapped by a Moldie heading for the Moon.

The Hero: It's a toss up between Randy and Tre, both of whose histories we get in detail. Stahn/Sta-Hi is back, in slightly more than a cameo rôle as a senator, and Cobb makes a brief appearance.

The Femme Fatale: Randy's mother's lesbian lover Honey seduces Randy, but his main love is a Moldie. Monique and Parvati can each be dangerous to him, by betraying him, killing him or taking him over.

Playing The Angles: The novel focuses on the development and use of a new kind of technology, the Moldie. The Moldies, being intelligent, have ideas of their own, and don't necessarily want to be so controlled; curiously both they and the Heritagists have the same goal, to get all Moldies off the planet Earth. The best place for them to go is a haven on the Moon.

The Style: The story focuses on eight of the characters, but is still told in the third person. Each of the chapters are dated, and the first half dozen deal with their overlapping and separate lives from 2031 (the defeat of the robots on the Moon) to the end of October 2053. The remaining ones deal with events in November and December 2053. Thankfully there are a number of family trees printed at the front of the volume to make the various relationships clear.

The Underworld: Death is still not the end, with Cobb back from the dead (again) and Wendy brought back a number of times as well as being cloned for food.

The Pay-Off: It's best to focus here on the individual chapters and the way they interrelate than the narrative as a whole, but Rucker is never less than inventive. Perhaps as a way of rounding out the climax he introduces a number of races of aliens to up the stakes for humanity (and the Moldies, for that matter). There is the kind of casual inventiveness of insignificant detail typical of Philip K Dick's *Ubik* (1969; compare that novel's lavish descriptions of outrageous costumes). It's worth pointing out that this novel includes a fair amount of sexual activities, but it's not particularly described in an erotic manner (or, not erotic to me, anyway).

Realware (2000)

The Set-Up: February 2054. Phil Gottner's father is missing, presumed dead, having fallen into a wuwu, a kind of klein bottle. At the funeral of what is left of him, Phil meets Yoke Starr-Mydol and falls in love with her. Yoke disappears off to Tonga, and meets up with the aliens (now labelled Metamartians) from the previous book. They give her an alla, a magic wand that conjures objects into being by transmuting atoms.

The Hero: Phil has had enough: he has lost a parent, and his girlfriend Kevvie is tripping all the time. (Cobb is still around, in limpware form, and is used to help Yoke travel to Earth from the Moon).

The Femme Fatale: Yoke is another independent spirit, but quick thinking enough to be able to save Cobb when he is poisoned with a drug.

Playing The Angles: The aliens which appeared briefly towards the end of *Freeware* are back, and have a bigger rôle to play here. The scope is widening out from the Earth and the Moon to a much more cosmic scale, just as the technology of information has shifted from digital to DNA to fungi to... well, the universe itself. At the same time, the focus is much tighter as Phil and Yoke are the centre of each alternate chapter.

The Style: Still very inventive, but less frenetic than the previous book. Indeed this is the most linear narrative in the sequence since *Software*. Given characters named Phil and Jane, and an alien-pig called a Wubwub, there seems to be a set of Philip K Dick references – his twin sister was called Jane, and pig-like wubs occur at various points in the collected works.

The Underworld: Phil goes into the hyperdimensional realm which seems to be a world of the dead – which has more than a whiff of Lewis Carroll and Edwin A Abbott's classic novel *Flatland* (1884).

The Pay-Off: As Arthur C Clarke should have had said, any insufficiently advanced sf is indistinguishable from fantasy. The wand which changes matter seems to be a magic wand, and the Sorcerer's Apprentice is mentioned to make this clear. Rucker's mathematical and cybernetic future shades into the fantastic, and it might be argued that the technology is far too advanced for half a century down the line. On the other hand, the most advanced technology is alien, and progress is speeding up.

Lewis Shiner

Shiner (1950-) was included in *Mirrorshades* with the story 'When Human Voices Wake Us,' which involved cloning, and had already written the novel *Frontera* which is viewed as cyberpunk. *Deserted Cities Of The Heart* (1988), a richer confection of Mexican-based magic realism, complete with sex, drugs and politics, comes highly recommended.

Frontera (1984)

The Set-Up: A decade ago, the Frontera colony on Mars was abandoned, but now Pulsystems is spearheading a mission to return there, for unknown reasons. Kane, nephew of Morgan, the director of Pulsystems, sees fellow astronaut Reese as a father and is suspicious of Takahashi, a vice-president also on the mission. Mars is not as dead as they were led to believe, and an implant in Kane's head may decide the fate of the colonists, and the mission.

The Hero: Kane is a hero who knows he is a hero, saturated as he is in Greek mythology and *Hero With A Thousand Faces*. Reese is a hero gone to seed, an astronaut on the earlier Mars mission who is returning to his past.

The Femme Fatale: Perhaps Molly, Reese's daughter, or Verb, his granddaughter, who knows more than she should – or Lena, the fourth member of the returning mission.

Playing The Angles: Two of the team know more about what they are heading into (and why they are on the mission) than they are letting on to the rest of the crew, and are keeping it quiet for their own reasons. Equally, their arrival is not unexpected, since the colony can listen into their radio communications; the colony has its own good reasons for keeping quiet. And then there's the second mission, a few days behind the first.

The Style: The narrative switches between a number of characters as we get to know their pasts on Earth, and learn the way that the world as we know it has collapsed, and the new world order (mostly involving multinational corporations) which has evolved to take its place. Kane's own narrative is somewhat fractured, with a certain lack of continuity, but perhaps that indicates his lack of control of his perceptions, or something...

The Underworld: Kane is seeking a cave, and name checks Orpheus and Eurydice.

The Pay-Off: Another astonishing debut novel from 1984, an annus fantasticus in science-fictional terms. It's a shame that Shiner has drifted away from sf, but his work is worth tracking down anyway.

John Shirley

A rock singer and writer born in 1954, his background in music informs much of his work, which spans horror and sf.

City Come A-Walkin' (1980)

The Set-Up: Here's a puzzler. Stu Cole becomes a vigilante, tracking down vigilantes, as well as Mafia types and the corrupt. He's told, if not forced, to do this by the City itself (himself?), which has decided to clean up San Francisco. The only thing is the City is suspicious that Stu's friend Catz will betray them, especially as she seems to want to persuade Stu that he's just being a puppet.

The Hero: Stu runs a night-club, which is doing all right, when he notices this mirror-shaded customer he nicknames City. Stu has a past, he used to be a burglar, and he becomes cold to the violence he has to commit very quickly, whilst protesting against committing it.

The Femme Fatale: Catz Wailen, real name Sonja Pflug, sings in a band which play in Stu's club. Because she has telepathic powers, her music is able to reach the clientele with a strange force. Like most cyberpunk heroines, she can take care of herself.

Playing The Angles: So far, the mean streets of a city (San Francisco, an unusual choice) and punk attitude, if not precisely a given youth movement. Stu has been around for a while. The particulars of the crowds – gay areas, sadists leading masochists around on leashes and other details – suggests it is extrapolating from a 1970s vision of the city (Watergate is invoked, and the criminal Mr Big has taped meetings, so the 1970s milieu is clear). There's also a sense of a cybernetic future: the idea of machines connecting across the world, a global village, and a call for letters to be sent electronically. E-mail was possible in 1980, but exceedingly rare.

The Style: The city is described as if it is alive (it is personified), but conversely the people are like machines; certainly they've lost autonomy over their actions. The book has a kind of distance to it, like horror.

The Underworld: San Francisco as a city of the dead, and Stu as being as good as dead without his credit rating. At the start and end of the book, Stu is a disembodied voice, suggesting a speech from beyond the grave.

The Pay-Off: A dark novel, with an all too plausible vision of the city of the future. With its punk ethos, its violence, its exploration of technology and information, the novel is clearly cyberpunk, and very good indeed.

The Song Called Youth trilogy (*Eclipse* (1985), *Eclipse Corona* (1988) and *Eclipse Penumbra* (1990)) is based around a musician, Rickenharp, whose influences are pre-punk: he is a rocker, with a taste for The Velvet Underground. The world is in a slow burn of a war, and an organisation called Second Alliance (SA for short) is exploiting the situation to its own ends, isolating a series of racial others. Rickenharp falls in with a motley array of resistance fighters in a derelict Europe, some of whom have infiltrated SA. If the city came alive in *City Came A-Walkin'*, here the city is dead. Meanwhile, up in orbit, a nearly complete space station is undergoing a coup and loss of political and social stability. Personally, I thought the first volume was a mess, with no plot developing in a satisfying manner, and lots of authorial digression as we are told the future history. Shirley has since revised these volumes. There are also short-story collections which are of interest, *The Exploded Heart* (1996), written much earlier, and a more solid collection, *Heatseeker* (1988). Most of Shirley's other work is in the horror genre.

James Patrick Kelley (1951-), author of the story 'Solstice' went on to publish two novels, *Planet Of Whispers* (1984) and *Look Into The Sun* (1989) about galactic communications, *Wild Life* (1994) and, with John Kessel, *Freedom Beach* (1985). Another writer to appear in *Mirrorshades* (with the story 'Stone Lives') was Paul Di Filippo, perhaps best-known for his three short novels collected as *The Steampunk Trilogy* (1995).

4. Post-Cyberpunk

The cutting-edge nature of cyberpunk ensured that it rapidly became a cliché: like many avant-gardes it was obsolete as soon as the mainstream media took notice of it. Indeed, some people began to argue that there had never been such a thing as cyberpunk – merely a collection of disparate writers linked together under a marketing label by the golden pen of Bruce Sterling. But computers, AIs, nanotechnology, hackers, prostitutes, junkies or assassins as heroes, multinational corporations, updatings of the Orpheus or Harrowing of Hell narratives and so on continued to be written about. Once *Reservoir Dogs* and *Pulp Fiction* had entered the public imagination, every new writer was labelled 'William Gibson crossed with Quentin Tarantino.' This chapter discusses some of the significant writers of what might be seen as post-cyberpunk.

Wilhelmina Baird

Baird, real name Joyce Carstairs Hutchinson, was born in Scotland in 1935, grew up in England and lives in France. She began publishing novels after she had retired from teaching. *CrashCourse* was followed by *ClipJoint* (1994), *PsyKosis* (1995) and *Chaos Came Back* (1996).

CrashCourse (1993)

The Set-Up: Professional burglar Cassandra Baines, male prostitute Dosh and aspiring sculptor Moke share a squat and dream of getting out of there. Their chance comes when they have the opportunity to star in a high-tech movie which records what they do, and what they feel; the only snag is they won't be given a script, and they're not certain all of them will make it out alive.

The Hero: Cass is resourceful and caring, and more than able to look after herself (and others) before the movie begins. Once the movie starts, she begins to be a jealous girlfriend.

The Femme Fatale: They find Mallore, a 16-year-old girl who has been abused by her father and take her in. Cass thinks she's acting, but Dosh is smitten by her. And any attempt by Cass to expose her will leave her even more in the jealous girlfriend rôle – and likely to be killed off

Playing The Angles: There is much talk early on about the clichés of narrative: the best friend who is killed off to legitimise the hero's actions, the lone female who makes it through in the end, the comic relief characters in the First Act. And to some extent this exposes the mechanism of the plot – with some comic relief characters, as well as friends being killed off as an excuse for later mayhem and violence.

The Style: Noirish is the word, with the mean streets of an imagined city predominating. A doctored cover quote from William Gibson on the British edition suggests that it is London, but the city feels very different and is referred to as Ashton.

The Pay-Off: In approved manner the lone hero(ine), with all the cards stacked against her, is able to see clearly and turn the tables against her enemies. (That's a dreadful mixed metaphor, but appropriate in the circumstances). The novel both uses and critiques the clichés.

Bruce Bethke

Headcrash (1995)

The Set-Up: Jack Burroughs (Jack – as in jack in; Burroughs – as in William Seward) is fired from his job with the corporation MDE, after an argument with his new (female) boss and goes back to the basement room of his mother's home. Hanging out as MAX_KOOL in an on-line club, Heaven, he is hired to steal some data from his old company, using a new higher-tech virtual reality suit. This he does with consummate ease, only to find that this is but a test of his skills before the real mission.

The Hero: Burroughs seems a bit of a loser in real life, and is sexually frustrated. Whilst his best friend and new business partner LeMat finds a girlfriend with whom he engages in energetic, long and frequent sexual behaviour, he remains celibate. Whenever he is about to jack into virtual intercourse, he is withdrawn from the net, or an event intervenes to prevent it.

Playing The Angles: Burroughs suffers homosexual panic when he puts on the VR suit. It is bad enough that he has to don a data bra and bikini, threatening his masculinity, but he also has to insert a Sacroiliac Neural Induction Device into his anus. LeMat certainly doesn't want to threaten his own masculinity by helping Burroughs with this aspect. Burroughs, caught in an ambiguity between penetration and the horror of being penetrated, spends much of the rest of the book being worried about this device. As this novel is a comedy, it is hard to decide whether this is endorsing the hero as sexually-terrified-asshole (as it were, almost literally) on some sort of unconscious level, or whether it is satirising this tendency. In this book, the entry into true experience of virtual reality, with smell and taste as well as the other senses, is by means of inserting this

ProctoProd into one's anus. Bethke cannot be serious. At the same time this is hardly gut-wrenchingly funny.

The Style: A running joke is the use of 'infonuggets' – boxed comments which give information about terms or characters mentioned in the text. The result is that the novel aspires to the condition of hypertext, and that Bethke does not have to disguise his infodumps when they happen, but make a virtue of them.

The Pay-Off: Whilst some of the gags are funny (the khyberpunks, who are an on-line teenage mujahedin community, a fabulously wealthy author bearing a starling resemblance to Michael Crichton, and vandals who improve the condition of Burroughs' car by getting him a new stereo and respraying the bodywork) there is a sense of infantilism about this novel. Nevertheless, he mixes cyberpunk clichés and stereotypes with a genuinely gripping plot to produce an entertaining whole. There is little which is original here, but that is hardly the point.

Simon Ings

Simon Ings was born in 1965, and began his career in the anthology *Other Edens III* (1989), before publishing in *Interzone*, *New Worlds* and *Omni*. His second novel *City Of The Iron Fish* (1994) has been compared to *Gormenghast* (1950) and to M John Harrison's *Viriconium* (1988); it should not be a surprise that he collaborated on a story with Harrison, 'The Rio Brain' (*Interzone* 104, February 1996). His first novel, however, is post-cyberpunk.

Hot Head (1992)

The Set-Up: Humanity has succeeded in building machines capable of replicating themselves, but has lost control of them. Malise Arnim was involved in fighting one of the early ones, the Moonwolf, and now Earth faces another invasion. And Malise, just possibly, has the information to stop them.

The Hero/Femme Fatale: Malise shows great prowess and ability in fighting others, and getting out of sticky situations. She is augmented with a data-fat, a means of linking to sources of information. This is illegal technology, which doesn't help Malise in her quest for a quiet life. Her sexual partners are predominately – but not exclusively – female. This is typical of the practice of a number of male British sf writers of the period – compare Geoff Ryman's (non-cyberpunk) *The Child Garden* (1987) and Colin Greenland's space opera *Take Back Plenty* (1990).

Playing The Angles: Writing in the early 1990s, Ings extrapolates a twenty-first century dominated by Islam, and uses both Europe and the Solar System as a setting. He moves from moments of great tenderness to explosions of violence or its aftermath.

The Style: The book begins with an account of Malise's childhood with her father (her mother having been assassinated), but abandons any sense of linear chronology after 40 pages into the book. It cuts between the latest threat and the fight against the Moonwolf, and luxuriates in an event experienced in a storytelling machine. The epilogue suggests that her life has been replayed (but not necessarily in the right order) by the self-reproducing machine her consciousness has entered.

The Underworld: The characters in the self-reproducing machine describe themselves as dead, and a nearby river has a hint of the Styx about it.

The Pay-Off: An ambitious, convoluted first novel, which is well written and repays close attention but is undeniably difficult. A number of chapters use Tarot cards for titles, but no explanation is given for this beyond the fact that some of the characters use such divination methods.

Hotwire (1995)

The Set-Up: Ajay is successfully working for the Haag, in part as an assassin, but he is discredited and ends up working for the mayor of Rio. The mayor wants Rio to come alive (apparently some of the cities are sentient), and so sends him to steal vital parts from Snow, an expert in AI and wiring. Unfortunately she is too strong for him, and he wakes, strapped to her operating table.

The Hero: Theoretically Ajay is strong, but we barely see him at his best. Once Snow has finished with him, his guts are wrecked, and he is cared for by Rosa, her daughter.

The Femme Fatale: Snow is another character we barely see, only learn about as an expert on the hot head technology. She has ensured that Rosa has a chip in her head, but a more developed version than seen elsewhere on the planet. Rosa is equally seductive, effectively (if unwittingly) masturbating Ajay on first meeting.

Playing The Angles: The Frankenstein story is a parallel here: Snow has various ghoulish experiments, and Ajay fears taking Rosa home in case the mayor experiments on her. Still, he is also doing some body work himself on his sister, so he can hardly complain. Who can you trust? Who is the true monster?

The Style: Dislocated. The narrative has great leaps (the blurb speaks of Ajay losing his job by being seduced but it isn't that straightforward) and cuts between different stages. It is still linear, but with leaps. Also intercut into the story are poetic bits and woodcuts (the latter by Simon Pummell), which add little to the novel.

The Underworld: Rosa is sort of rescued from the underworld, but she also helps her rescuer to escape.

The Pay-Off: Too complex for its own good, and the weakest of the cyberpunk books by Ings.

Headlong (1999)

The Set-Up: Christopher and Joanne Yale were fitted with hardware to help them work as architects on the Moon. Having been made redundant, and had their hardware removed, the couple split up. Both of them suffer from Epistemic Appetite Imbalance, due to the withdrawal of extra senses. Now Joanne is dead, from murder or suicide, and Chris wants to know why.

The Hero: Chris is the viewpoint character, who falls in and out of love with Joanne and wants to find out the truth. (He feels like a murder suspect, so in a sense he is trying to clear himself. On the other hand, he suffers from the same condition as Joanne and no doubt fears going the same way if it is suicide).

The Femme Fatale: Joanne's search for pirated software and hardware, including a visit to the Mafia, leads Chris into dangerous areas, and her association with some illegal wetware puts him at risk from the attentions of the EU detectives in The Hague.

Playing The Angles: The world this is set in features a Britain split between a monarchist London which has seceded from the European Union, and a republic with a capital in Leeds. References to William Haig (sic) and Michael Portillo seem to lend an incongruent air of satire to the world building – much of which is set around the revived Docklands of East London.

The Style: Like *Hot Head* the narrative is told in fragments, although it is much more straightforwardly a series of memories in the present (although one looked back on from Leeds, probably after the end of the novel). London is a much more rural environment than might be expected, but this is the result of earlier troubles.

The Underworld: Again there is the sense that the post-human is a position of death, in other words beyond life.

47

The Pay-Off: The feeling of loss throughout the novel is palpable, but we never really get to see what the Yales had been able to experience with their post-human senses. There is a point when Chris' senses are revived, and this is suitably beyond mere human comprehension, but largely the reactions to the removal of the hardware can be perceived as a metaphor for grief.

In his most recent novel, *Painkillers* (2000), Simon Ings moves away from sf, although the mysterious boxes at the heart of the narrative are clearly invented technology. The action cuts between gruesome events in London and gruesome events in Hong Kong - it would probably appeal to anyone who likes John Woo movies - and features the triads. Fellow writer Kim Newman has a cameo rôle as a film critic.

Richard Kadrey

Kadrey (b. 1957) is a writer of fiction and non-fiction (he assembled the *Covert Culture Sourcebook: A Guide To Fringe Culture* (1993)), as well as an artist and rock musician. *Metrophage* (1988) was one of the 1980s sequence of Ace Science Fiction Specials, which had earlier included *Neuromancer*, as well as Kim Stanley Robinson's *The Wild Shore* and Lucius Shepherd's *Green Eyes* (all 1984). Kadrey's other novel is *Kamikaze L'Amour* (1995).

Metrophage (1988)

The Set-Up: In a near-future Los Angeles, Jonny Qabbala is having a bad time: a drug-dealer seeking revenge on Easy Money, he finds himself arrested by Committee for Public Health – a body he once worked for. Colonel Zamora gives him a choice: be beaten up and blinded by his men or act as a spy and get to know the super-dealer Conover.

The Hero: Jonny seems witty enough, and can talk himself out of a crisis, but most of the novel he doesn't quite know what's going on. His motivations are staying alive, seeking revenge, and keeping his girlfriend alive.

The Femme Fatale: Jonny is in a triangular relationship with Sumi – who steals electricity for people – and Ice – a prostitute who deliberately gets infected in order to sell her blood to make antibodies.

Playing The Angles: The world is split among new factions – especially the Arabs and the New Palestinians who had oil and petroleum when the rest of the world had run out. The US seem to be bolstering its undercut position by keeping its citizens oppressed. Meanwhile a new disease is hitting town – comparable to leprosy, but spreading like a virus. And then there's the mysterious alien race, the Alpha Rats.

The Style: Raymond Chandler once wrote that when he was in any doubt how to proceed, he would have a man come in through the door with a gun. Kadrey tries something similar here: at the end of virtually every chapter, and even in the middle of some of them, Jonny is knocked out and captured by another faction. Nobody ever seems to want to kill him, or if they do, they don't seem particularly capable of doing so. This can get a bit tedious, but is presumably meant to be a comic device. Not only do we not know where Jonny is going to end up, nor does Jonny himself, and it becomes less and less clear whether he is working for Zamora, pretending to work for Zamora, actually an anarchist, allied with the Alpha Rats (but lying about this or having forgotten it) or simply seeking revenge.

The Underworld: Los Angeles as hell? Stretching it I guess.

The Pay-Off: A black comedy of cyberpunk cliché or pastiche, with plug in eyes as perhaps the only real concession to the cyber. The violence is curiously distanced, as it is in so many Hammett and Chandler novels.

Kim Newman

Kim Newman (b. 1959) began publishing his first stories in *Interzone*, but has a parallel career as a film critic. He has written books on horror (*Nightmare Movies: Wide Screen Horror Since 1968* (1984)), westerns (*Wild West Movies* (1990)) and sf films about the end of the world (*Millennium Movies* (1999)). Much of his writing is a kind of rewriting classic horror fiction by supplementing it with real and fictional characters; he has written a number of alternate histories with Eugene Byrne. Whilst the novels and short stories have great entertainment value, there is perhaps the sense that Newman is a little too clever, or is shuffling together a random set of fictional characters.

The Night Mayor (1989)

The Set-Up: Daine, a master criminal, has been banished to a virtual reality realm where he seems to have become a creator rather than just an observer. Tom Tunney, award-winner designer of VR environments for entertainment, has been sent in to kill Daine, and has apparently gone native. Now Susan Bishopric, Tunney's major rival, is sent in too.

The Hero: We only really know Tunney when he is in the virtual city, where it is always 2:30 in the morning and always raining. He appears to be the standard gumshoe, except that he doesn't like such a term. Daine is dead, killed by an unknown hand, and yet the VR continues rather than ending; even worse, Tunney, like scores of private eyes before him, now has to keep one step ahead of the cops who think he is responsible.

The Femme Fatale: Susan is described in the third rather than the first person, and so we don't get quite as close to her, but we can feel the rivalry she feels with Tunney.

Playing The Angles: The virtual city is the Los Angeles of 1940s *films noirs*, with Humphrey Bogart, Sidney Greenstreet, Elisha Cook Jr, Joseph Cotten and others mentioned or playing cameo rôles. Whilst Tunney has a clear task to follow as a private eye – finding clues, being knocked out, arguing with the police – Susan is much more limited in the parts she can play beyond *femme fatale*. However, there is a choice between Mary Astor (*The Maltese Falcon*) or Lauren Bacall (*Casablanca*) and so on.

The Style: Rarely in cyberpunk have the streets been so tastefully mean; the Hollywood Hays Code which censored films here limiting quite how bloodthirsty Newman is able to be. Some films are precisely name checked, others are left as an exercise to the reader to identify.

The Underworld: The computer that runs the world is called Yggdrasil, hinting at Norse mythology somewhat at odds with the mythology of Hollywood's past.

The Pay-Off: A richly flavoured brew of film noir and cyberpunk, in some sense following through the cliché of Hammett and Chandler flavoured cyberpunk, in others allowing an update of such narratives.

Marge Piercy

He, She And It/Body Of Glass (1991)

The Set-Up: Having lost custody of her son in Y-S, Shira Shipman moves to Tikva to be with her grandmother, Malkah. Malkah is working on a project to build a cyborg with former lover Avram, and thinks that Shira may be the perfect person to complete their creation Yod's education.

The Hero: Shira is, we are told, good at her job, although she has not progressed as you'd expect. She also seems to be defined by her romantic attachments – or failures – with Gadi, Avram's son, with her ex-husband and now with Yod.

The Femme Fatale: Yod is potentially violent, but the combined forces of the love of good women and then fatherhood seem enough to tame the savage beast, although the violence is always just submerged. He simply doesn't know his own strength. (Why cyborgs are by definition violent isn't explained, but all previous creations seem to be male.)

Playing The Angles: Piercy acknowledges the influence of Gibson and cyberpunk, and the essay 'A Manifesto For Cyborgs' by Donna Haraway, which having analysed female cyborgs in various texts ends with the line 'I'd rather be a cyborg than a goddess.' Here it is better a cyborg than a god, but despite determinedly matriarchal societies (and the criticism implicit in the depiction of almost all the male characters), it shies away from developing the all-female or lesbian societies whose existence is mentioned. And Ari, for a while, clearly needs a father, but it has to be the father of the mother's choosing. I mean this as a disappointment that Piercy hasn't pushed her future further, rather than as a rejection of matriarchal societies.

The Style: The present day (twenty-first century) events alternate with Malkah's tale to Yod of the story of the Golem in 1600 Prague. This sets us up for knowing how Jewish societies (of which Tikva is merely the latest example) treat artificial beings. It thus enriches the novel – or belabours the obvious.

The Underworld: With its anti-Semitism and corporatism, Y-S is a hell, from which Shira first escapes and then has to return to in order to rescue her son. One minor character is called Lazarus, and a couple of others appear to come back from the dead.

The Pay-Off: This novel controversially won the Arthur C Clarke Award, when it was felt that Kim Stanley Robinson's *Red Mars* was a more important novel and, politically more crucial for the award, any future edition of the book would acknowledge the award. Piercy, despite having written a classic feminist dystopia in the form of *Woman On The Edge Of Time*, was considered an outsider, and it does show in the writing of this novel. *He, She And It* is a long book, and could have been told in half its length; on the other hand, it could be seen as leisurely. In a sense, *Terminator II* does this much better.

Justina Robson

Silver Screen (1999)

The Set-Up: Anjuli O'Connell, and Roy and Jane Croft met at a school for geniuses, and forged an uneasy friendship. Years later, Roy and Anjuli are working on a space station with an ultra-intelligent computer, 901, when Roy dies. Is it suicide, or murder? And has it got anything to do with an upcoming court case set to rule whether or not AI computers are sentient? Anjuli has to find out, and discover what Roy was working on, aided by messages from Roy from beyond the grave, and 901 itself, before those who are trying to kill her succeed.

The Hero: Anjuli is the central narrator of all but one chapter, and comes from joint Irish and Punjabi stock. Her claim to fame is a photographic memory, a feature that lies unused until late in the novel.

Playing The Angles: The Silver Screen is the gap between human and AI consciousness, but it is also a reference to cinema. Many of the clues that Anjuli receives are in the form of characters from films, as hologram extensions of the computer. Like Kim Newman's characters in *The Night Mayor*, the figures are from *noir* staples such as *The Maltese Falcon*, as well as *The Blue Angel* and *Casablanca*. On the other hand, some of Roy's clues take a determinedly low-technological form – paper notes, a comic book, a hand-written diary. It's also worth noting that it is the non-technological locations that are best evoked, with a minimum of prose: it is a book rooted in the landscapes of Yorkshire and the north of Britain.

The Style: Anjuli is the narrator of the bulk of the narrative, aside from an excursion of a friend to a robotic demolition derby. It's there to set up a later aspect of the narrative, but it's the one step wrong in the whole novel.

The Underworld: Roy speaking from beyond the grave, even the sense that he might be alive in another computer – and right at the end, a reference to Orpheus.

The Pay-Off: A powerful debut novel, steeped in the tradition of British sf and cyberpunk, without being a slavish adherent to such a legacy. The novel was shortlisted for the BSFA and Arthur C Clarke Awards (Ken MacLeod's *The Sky Road* won the former, Bruce Sterling's *Distraction* won the latter), so she is clearly a name to watch.

Neal Stephenson

Neal Stephenson began publishing novels with a campus novel *The Big U* (1984), which seems unlikely to be republished but has been pirated on-line. He followed this up with *Zodiac*, subtitled an eco-thriller, which depended on chemistry and spin to deal with pollution in Boston. But it was with *Snow Crash* that Stephenson came to prominence.

Snow Crash (1992)

The Set-Up: Hiro Protagonist, freelance hacker, expert swordsman and pizza deliverer for the Mafia, in a near-future America, discovers that a new drug and computer virus is infecting hackers. A floating community of refugees may be threatening America.

The Hero: Hiro is multi-talented, but is the asshole as hero, and spends much of the novel hanging around in cyberspace (here, the metaverse) researching the virus and Sumerian mythology. In fact the world is saved by...

The Femme Fatale: YT, a 15-year-old skateboarder, who falls in love with and defeats Raven. Also bear in mind her dentata, which injects a hypodermic needle into the penis of anyone who tries to rape her.

Playing The Angles: This is Gibson played partly for laughs, with the power fantasies of geeks being played for real: in the metaverse you can be Clint Eastwood or a talking penis. Such fantasies may well be undercut by YT's abilities, but it still feels a bit ambiguous. The near-future America is one which has fragmented into small communities which defend their borders – rather like in Ken MacLeod's *The Cassini Division*.

The Underworld: The Librarian tells Hiro the Sumerian myths of Inanna, the Queen of Heaven who enchanted Enki the God of Wisdom and made off from his palace in the watery fortress with divine knowledge and laws. Inanna is later imprisoned in the Netherworld. She is rescued, along with ghosts and ghouls. The watery fortress is the Raft, but Hiro begins by hacking the metaverse.

The Style: The long digressions are fun, especially the conspiracy theories and the speculation about language, but they slow down a frenetic pace.

The Pay-Off: A novel which combines satires and cyberspace, but seems blind to the racism of its hordes of Asian masses.

Interface (1994)
(with J Frederick George as Stephen Bury)

The Set-Up: How do you follow up an internationally best-selling cyberpunk novel? By co-writing a political thriller with your uncle under a pseudonym, stupid. Senator William Cozzano suffers a stroke, and is given a revolutionary treatment: a chip is implanted in his brain, to replace destroyed neural pathways. This becomes crucial when Cozzano runs for President in the 1996 race – his speech can be remote-controlled by stimulating the correct part of his brain. Meanwhile, a hundred demographically selected Americans have been given televisions the size of a wrist-watch, and their reactions to political events can be monitored, and Cozzano's behaviour adjusted accordingly.

The Hero: Cy Ogle, who offers to represent the Cozzano family to the media, and who obviously has his own hidden agenda, is another in the line of asshole protagonists. Wise to media tricks, and certainly with more than few tricks up his sleeves himself, Ogle is always repellent and always right.

The Femme Fatale: Mary Catherine, Senator Cozzano's neurologist daughter, and Eleanor Richmond, a tough talking, no-nonsense African-American, who had worked for a right-wing senator and who then joins the election campaign.

Playing The Angles: America's financial debt as a country has to be bankrolled by someone, the money has to come from somewhere. And those someones, the Network, want a return on their investment, or to foreclose on the loan. And how better to foreclose on a loan than to take over the company loaned to? In other words, to bankroll a presidential candidate in order to take over the United States...

The Style: The information dumps which slowed down the action of *Snow Crash* are here in the early chapters. As each new character is introduced, we get their life history. We are told rather than shown, but told with such wit that we barely care.

The Pay-Off: Beyond the chip, which just about elevates itself above the level of the MacGuffin, nothing here is impossible with our current state of knowledge. However, after the various senilities of Reagan, Bush and Quayle, a presidential candidate on autopilot seemed to be a relief. Despite its length, this novel is never less than compulsive reading. The plot's disparate elements weave together satisfyingly, and ultimate fates are sealed with relish, and even with justice. If the ending is obvious from early on, the way it is achieved is a genuine surprise.

The Diamond Age
or, A Young Lady's Illustrated Primer (1995)

The Set-Up: In the neo-Victorian world of the twenty-second century, John Percival Hackworth is employed to design an educational primer for Princess Charlotte. He also makes one for his daughter, and a third which is stolen and ends up in the hands of Nell, the child of a broken relationship. Nell, like the other two girls across the social divide, begins to learn about her world and what she is capable of.

The Hero: Compared to other Stephensonian protagonists, Hackworth is underdeveloped, and lacking in something. For failing to cooperate with the authorities he is given a ten-year sentence, which covers a gap in the narrative, and the quest he acquires during the way seems underplayed. Other leading male characters are Judge Fang and Constable Moore, who fade away from importance as the narrative progresses.

The Femme Fatale: The resourceful Nell is the centre of the narrative, as her experiences and her knowledge alternate with accounts of various other inhabitants of the Victorian world. Her skill with knives and her body as a weapon comes in very useful.

Playing The Angles: The opening features exactly the sort of cyberpunk character we'd expect: clad in black leather, on the wrong side of both the law and organised crime, and enhanced with implants and weapons beneath his skin. But before the clichés can build up, he is written out, having been but part of a prologue to the quasi-Victorian novel Stephenson is writing. It's not quite cyberpunk, since the patriarchal Victorian family is balanced with the late twentieth-century style dysfunctional one, and the East End setting and airships aren't used enough. Meanwhile the presence of a character named Miranda (who provides the voice of the primer) and the power of books, especially the need to steal books, hint at *The Tempest*.

The Style: There is a mixture of registers here, most notably the fairy-tale voice of the primer, relating the adventures of Princess Nell.

The Underworld: Right at the end a relative is rescued from the underworld.

The Pay-Off: A curious example of a book with too many ideas. After the balkanised world of *Snow Crash* here it is empires (Atlantis – presumably North America and Europe but not the Vatican – China, Japan), but the political system remains unclear. The nanoorganisms as forensic clues, evolutionary tool, deadly weapon and so on are interesting, but still undeveloped. The sub-plot of thousands of kidnapped babies also seems to go nowhere. Stephenson is never less than interesting, but this lacks the scope and drive of almost any of the other novels.

Stephenson then wrote another novel with his uncle as Stephen Bury, *Cobweb*, but this was a Gulf War satire. His next project was the polemical *In The Beginning Was ... The Command Line*, an account of different operating systems for computers. His next novel, *Cryptonomicon* (1999) is only borderline sf, either in the sense of an alternate history of the cryptoanalysis of the Second World War or in the idea of setting up 'data havens,' private computer realms, in the present day. Lawrence Pritchard Waterhouse is working alongside Alan Turing at Bletchley Park and in America on cracking various codes, whilst in the field Bobby Shaftoe tries to keep their success a secret. Waterhouse and Turing realise they are working against their old friend Rudy, who may have codes of his own, including one called Arethusa. In the present Randy Waterhouse is setting up a place where data may be safely stored in encrypted form in South East Asia, and bumps into an ancient and international conspiracy, in part linked to cryptography, in part linked to massive amounts of gold hidden since the Second World War. The novel is the first part of a trilogy.

5. Cyberpunk-Flavoured Fiction

Not only was there still cyberpunk after the death of cyberpunk (post-cyberpunk), so there were works of fiction which felt like cyberpunk, read like cyberpunk, but nonetheless either lacked computers or punk characters. By analogy with chocolate-flavoured, these fictions can be read as cyberpunk-flavoured. Greg Egan, for example, is more usually dealing with scientist characters, but uses the figure of the post-human as interestingly as Sterling.

Greg Egan

A part-time computer programmer, Egan is Australia's leading living sf writer and probably the best-known writer from down under (Russell Blackford, Terry Dowling and Paul Collins have all written cyberpunk; a good taster to the work of contemporary Australian sf writers is the anthology *Dreaming Down-Under* (1999), edited by Jack Dann and Janeen Webb. Egan, perhaps wishing to be viewed as a writer rather than an Australian, is not in the collection.)

Quarantine (1992)

The Set-Up: Earth has been isolated from the rest of the Universe, in a bubble the size of the Solar System. Nick Stavrianos, an ex-cop, is called in to investigate the disappearance of Laura Andrews from a locked room. He traces her to Hong Kong, then relocates to Northern Territory, Australia, and falls into a scientific experiment that could change the world.

The Hero: Stavrianos is modified, with various add-ons and pieces of hard and software which help him do his job. Of course, these can turn against him and make him a tool of his own software.

The Femme Fatale: His wife, Karen, had been killed in an explosion, and he has dealt with his grief by using her personality in a piece of his software. She maintains a mind of her own, as it were, and criticises his actions.

Playing The Angles: It starts with an augmented human making his way through a noirish mission to track down a missing patient called Laura (compare how many daughters of the rich go astray in noir and hard-boiled fiction) and then shifts to quantum mechanics. Egan has his characters explain the famous thought experiment about a cat that may be dead or alive in a box (have you ever tried putting a cat in a box? you'd know if it were alive or not) to bring us up to speed, and explain how an event can go one way in this universe, reality or whatever, and another way in another. There's also the implications of Heisenberg's Uncertainty Principle to consider and how the act of observation fixes reality. And clearly all of this has something to do with the bubble which is masking out the stars.

The Style: Private eye time again, but with brand name dropping as we find out the title and price of each model of modification Nick has. At the same time, Egan never describe anyone's appearance.

The Underworld: Karen has some form of afterlife as a piece of software.

The Pay-Off: A book that literally makes the mind boggle, and one of the many remarkable debuts of cyberpunk (except that Egan's first novel was called *Bending The Angles*, and it wasn't sf). Well worth a look.

Permutation City (1994)

The Set-Up: In the future, the rich are able to make Copies of themselves on computer, in order to survive beyond their death. The experiences of the Copies is limited by the processing speed of the computer they are stored upon. Paul Durham, who has experienced 'life' like a Copy, is designing a mathematical, computer-generated realm which will be the promised land for Copies, where processing speed is unlimited.

The Hero: Paul Durham is effectively a god in the way he has created a new universe, but he loses control of the direction it goes in. He commits suicide on the apparent success of his creation, since he has a Copy to exist in his stead.

Playing The Angles: Cyberpunk, physics, philosophy: this is a complex novel where two different realms of reality are presented: a base reality and a computers-generated realm which seems much more Edenic than the standard rainy city cyberspace. We have two versions of a number of the characters: both the Original and the Copy. In one sequence a Copy of Paul Durham experiences life at different speeds – or perhaps (it is deliberately unclear) it could be the Original experiencing it. So, are the two versions really the same or are they different people – are the Copy's experiences more or less authentic than the Original's?

The Style: The thing you notice after a while is that Egan is better at describing the realm of the post- or trans-humans than describing the humans themselves: rarely, if ever, do we get a physical description of an individual.

The Underworld: The new realm is described as being beyond death – effectively a means of escaping the cycle of birth and death. Although, ironically, some Originals outlive the Copies.

The Pay-Off: Egan is one of the stars of the 1990s, and this is arguably his best novel to date. Read it. And then seek out his later novels (*Distress* (1995), *Diaspora* (1997) and *Terenasia* (1999) which explore the post-human, and his two short-story collections, *Axiomatic* (1995) and *Luminous* (1998)).

Jon Courtenay Grimwood

Jon Courtenay Grimwood was born in Malta but is now resident in London, where he works as a freelance journalist.

neoAddix (1997)

The Set-Up: Clare Fabio is fired from her rôle as police prosecutor after a multiple murder, including the assassination of the American Ambassador, Mayer. She is contacted by Makai, a computer construct in search of its identity, once the property of Mayer. She is told to track down Alex Gibson, an evidence chaser whose implanted camera has picked up data that will radically alter a trial which is under way.

The Hero: The first appearance of Alex is as a crucified body, but this doesn't stop him being a character. He is off stage for much of the novel, the central character being Clare.

The Femme Fatale: Razz is a half-caste hacker who gets involved in tracking Alex down.

Playing The Angles: The punk characters – Razz, Johnnie T the leader of the Japanese gang neoAddix – and the post-humans – Alex, who gets rebuilt, Makai – situate the novel as being cyberpunk, but a rather daft plot about 800-year-olds seeking bodily immortality has been tagged on. Oh, and a character is called *Gibson*. Perhaps a homage? Could 'Alex' be an echo of *A Clockwork Orange*'s narrator? And a line (echoing an Arthur C Clarke story, 'The Nine Billion Names Of God') about the stars going out is another. Intertextuality or lack of originality?

The Style: There is great relish in the descriptions of violence, medical operations, boy murderers and boy victims.

The Underworld: A crucified figure comes back from the dead... and he's not the only one. The book opens with two epigraphs about death and life.

The Pay-Off: It's a first novel, of course, but it's still a bit of a mess, feeling as if it's been assembled from a number of related novellas. Gibson vanishes as Clare takes over, then Clare fades from view. Maxine occurs a couple of times early on and then disappears until much later.

And so on. Clearly Grimwood's setting up things for later, but it's still hard to follow.

Lucifer's Dragon (1998)

The Set-Up: In the twenty-first century Passion DiOrchi uses her trust fund and her family's tremendous wealth to built a replica of Venice in the Pacific – neoVenice. A hundred years later the construction is part of the multinational media corporation CySat, and ruled by a prepubescent Doge. The Doge is murdered, and suspect number one is the daughter of one of the council who really runs things.

The Hero: In some ways Angeli, the policeman who is investigating the crime, but perhaps also Passion (although female) whose resourcefulness built the city.

The Femme Fatale: Razz is back (as indeed is Alex) but this time she's in a different body.

Playing The Angles: The question of 'why?' doesn't seem to be answered – why Venice rather than anywhere else, why a ten-year-old Doge, why characters get dropped from the narrative not having done anything... It's a police procedural but, rather like *NYPD Blue*, which is frequently alluded to, Angeli alights on his man at once and just has to interrogate the suspect for long enough.

The Style: Again there is pleasure in describing sex and violence, but not so much, and again characters come and go.

The Underworld: Death is not the end. The title of the video game which is also a weapon, Lucifer's Dragon, suggests an underworld connection.

The Pay-Off: Still struggling to keep control; Alex is some kind of guru figure in deepest Africa, but is barely given anything to do. Razz shows signs of life but is stuck in a sub-plot. It's a sequel to *neoAddix*, it's better written, but still a difficult read.

reMix (1999)

The Set-Up: Lady Clare Fabio's daughter LizAlec has been kidnapped and Fixx Valmont has been set to try and track her down and rescue her. Meanwhile the Third Napoleonic Empire in France is under siege from the Fourth Reich, and a virus is eating its way through the steel of Europe.

The Hero: Fixx, a former music star, has fallen on hard times, having been imprisoned for the alleged statutory rape of LizAlec. He also lacks his full complement of limbs. Nevertheless, he is able to make good progress in tracking down his one-time girlfriend.

The Femme Fatale: LizAlec has somewhat rebelled against the dainty life perhaps expected of a princess-type figure. Whilst she isn't invulnerable, she's pretty good at taking care of herself and turning male aggression against itself.

Playing The Angles: By now Alex is a god and Razz doesn't seem to be far behind. These two characters show up in relation to a minor plot strand, an ark being built by a religious cult. In this novel the religious, political and social flavour of the world seems much better and more clearly thought through.

The Style: In general the narrative flows much better, largely ping-ponging between the narrative arcs of LizAlec and Fixx, but also developing the backgrounds of minor characters, and filling out Lady Clare ambiguous rôle as politician and mother. There is still graphic sex and violence, but it seems less gratuitous, and characters at least seem to get their come-uppance for their moral infringements (mind you, so does everyone else). The epigraph is taken from William S Burroughs, and a name of a spaceship – *The Shockwave Rider* – borrows a John Brunner title.

The Underworld: Perhaps only in the figure of Alex as god.

The Pay-Off: This is less cyberpunk than the first two volumes, although an AI and augmented humans do play major rôles. The punk element is perhaps much more to the fore. It is head and shoulders above Grimwood's first two novels, and is in some ways reminiscent of Jack Womack's fiction.

redRobe (2000)

The Set-Up: Axl Borja has been sent by Cardinal Santo Ducque to a space habitat called Samsara. His mission relates to the death of Pope Joan and millions of dollars which have vanished from the Vatican coffers. On Samsara he comes across Mai, a kidnapped Japanese prostitute who has been told she is Joan.

The Hero: Axl is an ex-assassin, under sentence of death, but who manages to get around this by agreeing to the off-world mission. He is resourceful, can talk his way out of a crisis, and once featured as a child in *WarChild*, a narrative broadcast by CySat.

The Femme Fatale: Mai is virtually helpless, with only her will left to her.

Playing The Angles: This is a loose sequel to the three earlier books – there is no mention of Alex Gibson, the plague, Razz or Clare. On the other hand, there is a reference to Lucifer's Dragon, CySat exists in this world, and Samsara is out beyond the Arc and run by Lars, a character from *reMix*. As the title might suggest, Samsara is a Buddhist enclave, which has an open door policy for refugees. The Buddhism is set up in opposition to the Catholicism (owners of the eponymous redRobe?) of the characters back on Earth, particularly in Mexico.

The Style: There is less sex and violence here, and even a strong thread of humour in the character of an intelligent Colt gun which gives advice to those who wish to use it. Abandoned by Axl, it eventually tries to find its way back to him (*The Incredible Journey*, anyone?) but since Samsara is a weapon-free zone and even Cardinal Ducque has scruples about abusing diplomatic immunity and the diplomatic pouch, it has to find its own way through the solar system.

The Underworld: A number of characters are suspended between life and death, perhaps reminiscent of the idea of resurrection in Catholicism or of reincarnation (or even the transmigration of souls?) in Buddhism.

The Pay-Off: The cover still compares Grimwood to Tarantino, but like the director he appears to have mellowed with experience: there is less dwelling on sex and violence. Or perhaps we're desensitised by now? The cyberpunk trappings – a couple of AIs, an ex-assassin, a Japanese prostitute – seem somewhat perfunctory, in what eventually emerges as a morality tale, although there is a twist in the tale about media coverage of events, and perhaps an echo of D G Compton's *The Continuous Katherine Mortonhoe*.

Gwyneth Jones

Gwyneth Ann Jones, who also writes books under the name Ann Halam, has a rich and varied body of work, covering children's, young adult and adult fiction, and horror, fantasy and science fiction. She is also one of the field's major critics, with a useful collection of non-fiction in the form of *Deconstructing The Starships* (1999). Her diptych, *Divine Endurance* (1984) and *Flowerdust* (1993), describes a far-future Earth (with more than a hint of south-east Asian about it) in which a manufactured human leaves her home when the computers which had kept her locked up have malfunctioned. *Flowerdust* is extended from an episode in *Divine Endurance* to an entire book. Arguably her most sustained work is the Aleutian trilogy – *White Queen* (1991), *North Wind* (1994) and *Phoenix Café* (1996) – the account of an alien invasion of Earth and its consequences. The aliens believe they are immortal – reincarnating when killed – and have a gender system which is confusing to human eyes. The first book features Johnny, a discredited journalist, befriended and then raped (or seduced) by what he took to be a female alien. The subsequent volumes depict the Earth's further interaction with the aliens and their departure, and the consequences of the rape.

Escape Plans (1986)

The Set-Up: A matriarchal dystopia run by computers is the setting. Humanity has discovered that they are alone in the universe, a universe which is finite in scope. Games designer ALIC descends from her life of luxury in orbit to what remains of the Indian subcontinent. She meets Millie Mohun, and loses her again, as rumours circulate that Millie is dead or, worse, the subject of scientific experimentation.

The Hero: ALIC, On ALIC 4R4 or Pioneer Aeleysi is female, although her sex is only specified on a handful of occasions. She is a complex character, unhappy with her lot; at one point she even deletes her identity from the computers. She has another human, Pia, as a pet, but treats her relatively well, until Pia is repossessed.

Playing The Angles: The length of a lifespan has extended; it is now about 130 years, with ALIC being in her 80s. Millie, on the other hand, is rumoured to be immortal, or an alien, or otherwise different from the average human.

The Style: Dense, with lots of acronyms and slang derived from them. Fortunately for the terminally lazy there is a glossary at the back, although many of the terms could just about be worked out.

The Underworld: ALIC is also Alice, and the descent to Earth is a trip down the rabbit hole. She descends in part to rescue Millie from this literal underworld; on the other hand there is the sense that Millie has descended to Earth to rescue humanity.

The Pay-Off: A difficult book, which needs attention paid to it; it shares the information density and love of jargon of early cyberpunk.

Kairos (1988, revised 1995)

The Set-Up: England, the near future. Britain is on the edge of collapse into a police state, an Islamic movement threatens world stability, and a fascist cult called BREAKTHRU may just about tip things over the edge. Otto has been given a canister of film by her friend James, unaware that it is actually a new drug, Kairos. As sinister forces gather to get it back, Otto's son Candide takes it to her former lover Sandy. Sandy soon realises, as war breaks out, that she is already hallucinating.

The Hero: OK, Otto is a mishearing of Otter, which is the nickname of the lesbian daughter of a Labour MP. Otto runs a woman's bookstore, and shares her life with Sandy, a working-class woman who is always just one step ahead of being caught committing benefit fraud. Their friends, the Nigerian actor James Esumare and his lover, schoolteacher Luci, were their contemporaries at Sussex University.

Playing The Angles: The drug works on a sub-atomic level, eliding the difference between perception of reality and reality itself; thanks to quantum mechanics it seems that you just have to be in the general vicinity of the drug for it to work rather than having to ingest it. The drug that alters reality recalls Philip K Dick's *The Three Stigmata Of Palmer Eldritch* (1964) and the strange ageing effect it has is reminiscent of the same author's *Ubik*.

The Style: Allusive – references to *The Jungle Book*, Narnia, Dante, Hardy, Hopkins and so on pepper the text, adding to the already poetic flavour of the piece. Not only do Sandy and Otto alternate between being the main character, but the viewpoint can shift midscene.

The Underworld: Britain itself is a hell, into which Sandy must descend to save it.

The Pay-Off: A typically rich brew from Jones, with a tightly extrapolated future Europe, told utterly convincingly, with a matter-of-fact twisting of reality added in for good measure.

Shariann Lewitt

Memento Mori (1995)

The Set-Up: The colony Reis has shut itself off from the rest of humanity thanks to a plague with no known cure. Mathematician Johanna is working on the epidemiology, and noting that the AI, RICE, who runs the colony's essential services is changing. Meanwhile the colonists try to get to grips with the situation of a colony dying out in the only way they see fit: by turning suicide into an art form.

The Hero: Johanna is the nearest the book has to a hero, since a number of characters appear to take a central part in the action, whether past or present. Johanna is mourning the loss of her son, and the subsequent abandonment by her husband. Peter Haas is a chess genius, challenging the AI's current favourite to a game.

The Femme Fatale: RICE is it, displaying a vein of cruelty, and perhaps not letting on all she knows. She is an AI designed from DNA, and able to learn from her experiences.

Playing The Angles: A peculiar mood permeates the novel, as various kinds of unusual arts are discussed, each of which seems to involve death. The clique which hang out in the Metz bar appear sometimes to be a group of punks, sometimes a group of spoilt students, an ambiguity common in real-life cyberpunk. And all the while the sense of finding patterns in chaos.

The Style: Poetic and fluid, with the viewpoint shifting almost imperceptibly between scenes.

The Underworld: The colonists are the not-yet dead.

The Pay-Off: An astonishing novel depicting a seamless, convincing world which is at once alien and a sensitive portrait of humans in an alien situation.

Jeff Noon

Jeff Noon had already won a playwriting competition before he sat down to write *Vurt*. The novel, his first, was published in 1993 by a new press called Ringpull. To their surprise, it was enormously successful and won the 1994 Arthur C Clarke Award and a poll of reviewers in the British Science Fiction Association magazine *Vector*. News of the novel spread by word of mouth throughout the British sf community, rather like a virus in its own right.

Vurt (1993)

The Set-Up: The novel is set in south-central Manchester, in particular in Rushulme, Moss Side and West Didsbury. The main characters are the Stash Riders, who take hallucinogenic Vurt feathers to obtain an experience which is part way between a drug trip and a computer game – a consensual hallucination. After taking a feather called Curious Yellow within a feather called English Voodoo, Desdemona disappears, and in her place as an exchange, there is the feather growing Thing-From-Outer-Space.

The Hero: Scribble, Desdemona's brother and lover and narrator of most of the novel. His narration alternates with the hints, tips, and evasions of Game Cat, which reads like a column from a computer games magazine.

The Femme Fatale: Only glimpsed at intervals though the novel, as Desdemona is in the Vurt.

Playing The Angles: The novel resembles nothing as much as an episode of *Scooby Doo*, written by William Burroughs.

The Style: Noon writes poetically, rhapsodising broken glass, dog dirt and the filth of Manchester.

The Underworld: Orpheus' wife Eurydike was bitten by a snake and died. Orpheus, a champion musician, then entered the underworld and won her back. And then, according to which version is being read, they left together or he broke the rules by looking back and lost her again. Some time later he is dismembered, and his head floated down stream, mourning and prophesying. Scribble is a musician, but is a DJ rather than a lyre player. He is the one who gets bitten by the snake, whilst in a Vurt hallucination. And finally, when he actually locates Desdemona, he releases her and stays behind himself.

The Pay-Off: The novel is framed with a boy taking a Vurt feather, so Scribble's rescue attempt leads to a Vurt within a Vurt or meta-Vurt, and when he takes another Curious Yellow feather, it becomes a meta-meta-Vurt. It is no wonder that realities on different levels are beginning to get confused. The Vurt which resembles the plot of the novel is described by the Game Cat as 'a bit like real life,' but there is no guarantee that Scribble's version is any more like real life. In fact, if the whole novel is a Vurt, then it is 'just a collective dreaming' and there is no guarantee that the information given about Vurt feathers is accurate, or rather, meant to be accepted as real.

Pollen (1995)

The Set-Up: In near-future Manchester the pollen count is rising, setting off hay-fever attacks, and bonding with the human reproductive system. This is leading to the potential for new hybrids between human and plant. Sibyl Jones begins by investigating a murder, and ends by entering the Vurt realm of Juniper Suction to defeat the invader, John Barleycorn.

The Hero: Having previously focused on a male, Vurt-feather using, anti-hero, Noon shifts our sympathies to the shadowcop Sibyl Jones. In *Vurt*, of course, Scribble and his friends had feared such hybrids. Sibyl is unable to use Vurt, being a dodo (that is, flightless), but she can ride other people's consciousnesses.

Playing The Angles: Before the novel proper there is an extract from *The Looking-Glass Wars* by R B Tshimoma, giving an account of the way dreams got coated onto a replayable medium, like the feather. This seems to situate the novel in the future history of these wars, and brings in an association with the Alice books, *Alice's Adventures In Wonderland* and

Through The Looking-Glass. Alice Hobart was the first investigator of the properties of Vurt. Noon also uses the traditional folksong 'John Barleycorn' (in a version by The Traffic) as an account of the strength of plants over humans (especially in whiskey or beer) and chooses a version in which John Barleycorn is triumphant.

The Style: This book is a lot less casually inventive than *Vurt*, with a growing sense of meaningful wordplay.

The Underworld: Manchester has its own cyberspace, the virtual map of the X-cab network. This is going to be replaced by a flower map, which will enable John Barleycorn to invade the world. Sibyl has to defeat him in his own realm, which is specifically designated as a realm of the dead.

The Pay-Off: A second novel never has the same impact as a successful first novel, and the structure here is odd, building to climax after climax. Noon is also shifting away from the urban blight of *Vurt*, and the escape into more pleasant Vurt realms, to a vision of a literary rural England.

His next novel *Automated Alice* (1996) is an updating of, or a 'trequel' to the Alice books, with Alice entering a 1998 Manchester from the nineteenth century, via a grandfather clock. 1998 has even more hybrids than the world of *Vurt* and *Pollen*, but these are mostly excuses for puns.

Nymphomation (1997)

The Set-Up: Manchester, 1999. A lottery-type game, Domino Bones, is being piloted: when the randomly altering domino they have bought matches up with that week's domino, cash prizes can be won. The game is run by one Mr Million, who appears to be one of the pupils in a 1949 class who were turned into mathematical geniuses by their teacher Miss Sayers. Jazir, an expert hacker, is being contacted by the missing Miss Sayers in the form of a computer virus, encouraging him to seek her in the House of Chances.

The Hero: Jazir the hacker, a character who allows Noon to take some note of the ethnic diversity of Manchester rather than simply using the hybrids as metaphors for race.

The Femme Fatale: Partly the figure of Miss Sayers, partly Celia (an anagram of Alice) who is on her own quest.

Playing The Angles: As well as the Asian-British community, Noon here depicts the homeless, university students and workers at a bookshop on Deansgate, a thinly disguised Waterstone's where he once worked. There is a greater sense of an integrated Manchester.

The Underworld: Again there is a quest into another realm – the Theseus Maze and the House of Chances – to rescue a lost female.

The Style: There is still a playfulness, for example in the way the recipes of Asian cuisine become an intrinsic part of the Vurt experience.

The Pay-Off: Again, not a match for the debut novel, but a distinct return to form. The details of the domino game (a satire on the British National Lottery) are a little unclear yet still allow Noon to refresh his metaphors.

Noon's next book was a collection of short stories, *Pixel Juice* (1998), including a number set at a tangent to the Vurt milieu; in one case, 'Ultra Kid And The Cat Girl,' there is the suggestion that the hybrids are the result of music recombining DNA sequences. The sequence as a whole has a number of discontinuities, and the presence in *Vurt* of a Vurt which seems similar to the narrative of that novel, plus the repeated image of a boy putting a feather into his mouth (at the start of *Vurt*, the end of *Nymphomation*) suggest that these narratives are themselves just feather narratives, each with its own origin myth. Having moved to Brighton, Noon now seems to have left Manchester and sf behind, shifting to rave culture in *Needle In The Groove* (2000).

Tricia Sullivan

Sullivan, an American resident in Britain, is the author of three sf novels to date, and a number of pseudonymous fantasy novels. Her first novel, *Lethe*, (1995) alternates between the narratives of Daire, who has travelled through a wormhole to an alien planet and Jenae, who has become part cetacean thanks to a virus. And then there are the Heads, brains in vats, who may know what is really going on. Sullivan's second novel is closer to cyberpunk.

Someone To Watch Over Me (1997)

The Set-Up: Croatia provides a suitably fresh and baroque setting for the opening, although before long the setting shifts back to New York apartments, and a more familiar future. Adrien Reyes is a trans, a channel for someone known only as C to view the world through. In Russia a mission to obtain some new technology called I is botched when Adrien is ambushed. Adrien has had enough: he escapes, bleeding, to Zagreb.

The Hero: Adrien is resourceful, good-looking, an expert in martial arts, and is somewhat spooked by the way C is trying to take him over.

The Femme Fatale: He meets an experimental musician named Sabina who is lured to America by C, while Adrien is having his implant removed.

Playing The Angles: Adrien is left trying to control his own identity once more, to penetrate the true identity of C, to protect Sabina (and her identity) and to survive the machinations of those searching for I.

The Style: The horror of having someone else in control of one's actions comes across, and the shift in focal characters means that often the reader knows more than the character in danger does, heightening both a sense of danger and of multiple personae. The handful of violent scenes do turn the stomach, as they should, but are never gratuitous

The Pay-Off: I did wonder about the precise mechanics of singeing scrotum hair when the possessor of said body part is hanging from the ceiling by his foot, and then decided I didn't need to know. In fact, forget I even brought it up.

Dreaming In Smoke (1998)

The Set-Up: The planet T'nane is inhospitable as a colony, given the amount of CO_2 in the atmosphere, and so the colonists are restricted to a precarious existence in an organic base, trying to solve the oxygen problem. Kalypso Deed rides shotgun as a scientist dreaming about the problem in virtual reality, with the assistance of the colony's AI, Ganesh. Unfortunately her client kidnaps her as an experiment and threatens the stability of the whole colony.

The Hero: Another female hero, not that she is particularly heroic other than by surviving. She is very passive, experiencing the actions of others rather than being a force in her own right.

Playing The Angles: Instead of actively creating a habitable planet, many of the characters are killing time, in the hope that it will all get sorted out. It's just a dream, aided by drugs, alcohol and a liberal usage of virtual reality. Kalypso is held in check, too, attending to the whims of others rather than colonising the rest of the planet.

The Style: To start with, the style is surreal, and there is a marvellous first sentence.

The Underworld: There are matriarchal beings known as the Dead who are outside in the wild landscape of T'nane.

The Pay-Off: Cyberpunk? Well, Kalypso has buckets of attitude at the start, the VR stuff offers the cyber, and some readers have seen the book as either cyberpunk or as a critique of cyberpunk. On the other hand, the author herself claims not to really know her sf, and any resemblance to the sub-genre is coincidental. The book won the 1999 Arthur C Clarke Award.

Jack Womack

Dryco

The Dryco sequence will consist of six books: *Ambient* (1988), *Terraplane* (1988), *Heathern* (1990), *Elvissey* (1993), *Random Acts Of Senseless Violence* (1993), and the book which completes the sequence, *Going, Going, Gone* as yet unpublished. Taken together, they form a future history of a New York dominated by the Dryco Organisation. Dryco was founded by Thatcher Dryden, who used to be a drug dealer. As the corporation rises, taking on competitors in the Soviet Union and Japan, so the country declines into violence. There are a number of attempts, mostly centred on Messiahs, to improve the morals of the company and the country, but these seem doomed to failure.

The order of the books is not the order of the events, with *Random Acts* charting in diary form the decline of a middle-class girl into poverty and madness in 1990s New York; Crazy Lola, as she becomes known, is referred to in the books written earlier. *Heathern* describes the power plays of Thatcher Dryden, from the point of view of his mistress, Joanna, and the attempt to use a miracle performing schoolteacher to sell salvation to the world. *Ambient* picks up the story a generation later, with Seamus O'Malley the Dryden Jr bodyguard falling in love with his mistress, Avalon, and being caught up in an assassination attempt. The novel ends poised on the edge of nuclear Armageddon. In *Terraplane*, Avalon and Seamus are in charge of Dryco, and are seeking some kind of device from the Russians. This device is accidentally triggered, sending the team back to an alternate 1939 where blues musician Robert Johnson hadn't died. *Elvissey*, set in 2033, uses this time travel device to kidnap Elvis Presley from the alternate 1954 in order to use him as a messiah. The final book is supposed to be set some time after this one.

The process of writing sequels and prequels allows Womack to explore the boundaries of his created world, enriching the life of a character killed off in a previous book, developing a theme. The sequence is not pure cyberpunk to the extent that it does not feature computers or cyberspace, to any large degree, although a super computer named Alice does play a part in some of the action. That being said, the structural rôle of cyberspace as a green space where problems in actual reality can be solved is taken here by the alternate or parallel pasts. The curious thing is that the pasts, being dominated by Nazis and right-wing racists, make the present day of the narrative actually seem preferable. Whatever else the faults of that present are, the problem of racism seems more or less under control.

From the start, Womack describes a world in desperate need of salvation, and one where salvation myths have great currency. In Macaffrey we have a messiah in contact with forces beyond the real world, but he is killed before Dryco can make use of this. The action remains in this world. In *Terraplane* and *Elvissey*, a trip is made to another realm, one in the past, which is in an entirely different universe, and thus must surely be of a different order of being. No matter how bad the realm of Dryco gets – and it gets pretty bad – this alternative realm is worse. With Churchill and Roosevelt dead, and Stalin assassinated, nothing stops Hitler in his march across Europe.

The visit here is surely one to Hell, from which Elvis is rescued. In both cases a messiah is sought, and with it a sense of transcendence, of something beyond this world – something perhaps we seek in sf, a conversation with the other, the radically different and strange. Of course it fails, it has to for the sake of the sequence. Book six is yet to come. If the world is saved, if Dryco regoods itself with the rest of the world, then the sequence has been closed.

6. Cyberpunk Goes To The Movies

Increasingly every big budget blockbuster seems to have a scene where characters receive or send e-mail, or surf the net or somehow have to beat a supercomputer which has a red LED digital clock counting down to zero... Some films have featured hackers as part of the plot – *The Net*, *Sneakers* and, er, *Hackers* - but I've chosen other titles.

Blade Runner (1982)

Director: Ridley Scott. Producer: Michael Deeley. Writers: Hampton Fancher & David Peoples, based on Philip K. Dick, *Do Androids Dream Of Electric Sheep?* Cinematographer: Jordan Cronenweth. Film Editor: Marsha Nakashima. Art Director: David Snyder.

Cast: Rick Deckard (Harrison Ford), Roy Batty (Rutger Hauer), Rachael (Sean Young).

The Set-up: Los Angeles, 2019. Six Nexus-6 replicants have returned to Earth and blade runner Deckard is assigned to retire four of them. He first has to prove he can distinguish Nexus-6s from humans by testing their creator's niece, Rachael. Rachael is a Nexus-6, but seems almost human, a factor Deckard must confront as he goes about his work.

The Hero: Deckard is a tough guy, divorced, resourceful, and yet barely seems a match for the superhuman Nexus-6s. He is beaten up, strangled, and has his fingers broken, all in the line of duty. And you get the feeling there's no pension plan.

The Femme Fatale: Rachael, narrow waisted, fur-trimmed collar, smoking, is a heroine straight out of film noir, and could be as dangerous as such a figure, but she is also naïve and has to be instructed to fall in love with Deckard by, er, Deckard. Still, she can handle a gun. And she's not as deadly as punkish Pris or exotic dancer Zhora, both of which are replicants.

Playing The Angles: The voice-over situates the film in noir territory, and not since *Metropolis* (1926) have the mean streets looked so futuristic. The special effects team, including Douglas Trumbull, have fashioned a convincing location from models, neon, smoke, real locations and sets, although ironically it looks like the Japan of the same director's *Black Rain* (1989). The villain, Roy Batty, is simply guilty of wanting longer life, and is not particularly fussy about how he gets the information, even going so far as to confront his father/creator.

The Style: Roy doesn't want to lose what he has seen, and a motif of eyes runs through the film, from the eye starring across the city at the start of the film to the eye manufacturer to a blinding to the eyes which may prove characters are really artificial, perhaps even Deckard.

The Pay-Off: A turkey on first release, the film has gained in credibility over the years and a small forest of trees has made way for articles about it. Clearly the film was a visual map for the location of much cyberpunk, and played with ideas of cyborgs, but it would probably be pushing it to say the film is cyberpunk. Certainly proto-cyberpunk is more convincing. The film had been altered after test screenings, with the voice-over being added and a happy ending of flying into the sunset tacked on. After the accidental screening of a test print in the early 1990s, a new version was assembled, closer to the original cut, with Deckard dreaming of a unicorn, proving he is a replicant as well (an idea already speculated about by fans and critics, given that Deckard is told six have escaped, and only five have been accounted for. Still, Deckard being number 6 (presumably not a free man) would make no sense of the narrative either; in fact the sixth was Mary, the all-American Mom, dropped from filming on grounds of dullness). The so-called *Director's Cut* (1992) replaced the original release, and balances the film more between Deckard and Roy (after all, if Deckard narrates, how can we see scenes which he is not present for?) In the summer of 2000, after months of speculation and rumour, British television showed a version which was closer again to the test-screening prints, restoring a visit by Deckard to the hospital to see a colleague, and apparently proving once and for all that Deckard *is* a replicant. Glad to get that one sorted out.

Videodrome (1983)

Director & Writer: David Cronenberg. Producer: Claude Héroux. Cinematographer: Mark Irwin. Film Editor: Ronald Sanders.

Cast: Max Renn (James Woods), Bianca O'Blivion (Sonja Smits), Nicki Brand (Debbie Harry), Brian O'Blivion (Jack Creley).

The Set-Up: Toronto cable TV executive Max is seeking cutting-edge porn when he stumbles across Videodrome, hard core material being beamed out from Pittsburgh. He meets Nicki Brand and the image of pundit Brian O'Blivion on a chat show, and introduces Nicki to Videodrome. Nicki is determined to appear on it. Meanwhile Max, troubled by hallucinations, begins to investigate Videodrome, and his path seems to lead him back to O'Blivion...

The Hero: Max only really has a handful of moods: excited by making money, puzzled by what's going on, then disgusted, then disgusted and puzzled as a hole opens up in his abdomen.

The Femme Fatale: Nicki initially appears as a feminist pundit, but almost immediately turns out to be game for anything, from being an object of lust to taking part in sadomasochistic practices.

Playing The Angles: Made just before the home computer revolution, the technology that causes characters to come adrift from reality is television not the Internet, with TV being more real than reality (as is the virtual world in cyberpunk being written a couple of years later). When a headset is placed over Max's head to measure his hallucinations, it looks rather like the helmets worn by those going into virtual reality. There's a level of paranoia behind the plot, however, which looks as much back to the 1970s thriller as it does to the suspicion of business and government in 1980s and 1990s cyberpunk. Never assume anyone has stumbled accidentally on anything: it could well be part of someone's plans for you.

The Underworld: Without giving too much away, the death of the body is necessary to go to the next level.

The Style: As so often in Cronenberg, the technology is organic in appearance and the body becomes mechanical – Max turns into a VCR.

73

Televisions bulge outwards, individuals reach into themselves and emerge with slimy hands. Visceral is perhaps the bon mot here.

The Pay-Off: Not cyberpunk as such, but a parallel case. Cronenberg was signed up to make the movie that eventually became *Total Recall* (1990) and made versions of books by Burroughs and Ballard. In other words, he seems to draw on much of the same influences as cyberpunk, but (with the possible exception of *eXistenZ*) puts a more biological spin on it.

The Terminator (1984)

Director: James Cameron. Producer: Gale Anne Hurd. Writers: James Cameron & Gale Anne Hurd. Cinematographer: Adam Greenberg. Film Editor: Mark Goldblatt. Art Director: George Costello.

Cast: The Terminator (Arnold Schwarzenegger), Kyle Reese (Michael Biehn), Sarah Connor (Linda Hamilton).

The Set-Up: In the future, machines and humanity are battling it out, with androids occasionally able to infiltrate human enclaves in disguise. The Terminator is sent back in time to try and kill Sarah Connor, who will somehow aid the human resistance in the future. Kyle Reese is sent back in time by the humans to protect her, and begins to fall in love with her.

The Hero: The Terminator can't help but be the centre of attention (Schwarzenegger's nude scene added to his female following) but the notional hero is Reese.

The Femme Fatale: Sarah spends a lot of the film being stalked or chased, and seems to have little control of her situation.

Playing The Angles: A low-budget film which was a huge hit, with a story eventually credited to Harlan Ellison. But equally it resembles stories by Philip K Dick ('The Defenders', 'Second Variety') where weapons have taken over from humanity. Whilst Dick went for the existential crisis, here the narrative is a cat and mouse chase, with Reese and Connor trying to keep a step ahead of their deaths.

The Underworld: In a sense the narrative is about changing the hell of the future.

The Style: Aside from the future sequences, the mood is surprisingly realistic.

The Pay-Off: Sarah is not so much punk as new romantic (as opposed to *Neuromantic*); this film can stand as one example of the present-day or near-future cyborg genre – compare *Robocop* (1987), *Universal Soldier* (1990) and hundreds of video premieres, with unstoppable killing machines or cops that are half-man/half-machine or, rarely, half-woman/half-machine.

Akira (1988)

Director: Katsuhiro Ôtomo. Producers: Shunzo Kato & Ryohei Suzuki. Writer: Izou Hashimoto. Cinematographer: Katsuji Misawa. Film Editor: Takeshi Seyama. Production Designers: Kuzuo Ebisawa & Yuji Ikehata & Koji Ono.

Cast: Shôtarô Kaneda (Mitsuo Iwata), Tetsuo Shima (Nozomu Sasaki), Kei (Mami Koyama), Ryû (Tesshô Genda).

The Set-Up: Neo Tokyo, rebuilt after a nuclear bomb, its streets inhabited by biker gangs and doomsday cults. Kaneda, leader of a gang, becomes concerned for his friend Tetsuo who has been involved in a government project, Akira. Tetsuo has become endowed with telekinetic powers, and threatens to destroy the city.

The Hero: The two friends Kaneda and Tetsuo are central to the narrative, and although he goes to the dark side, Tetsuo has impressive powers.

The Femme Fatale: Kai is an independent heroine, active rather than passive, although she does have to be rescued by Kaneda.

Playing The Angles: An anime based on the best-selling manga by Katsuhiro Ôtomo, it falls into the all-too-neat history of Japanese movies about fear of nuclear mutation (see all the Godzilla movies). It's a complex movie, with an ambiguous ending, and it's streets ahead of anything Disney have produced.

The Style: Fast, frenetic but with really impressive backgrounds that are the best cityscapes in sf since *Blade Runner*.

The Pay-Off: If you see just one anime, this might as well be it. It's the film which has had most coverage, and I think it rewards the attention.

Tetsuo: The Iron Man (1988)

Director: Shinya Tsukamoto. Producer: Shinya Tsukamoto. Writer: Shinya Tsukamoto. Cinematographers: Kei Fujiwara & (surprise!) Shinya Tsukamoto. Film Editor: (can you guess?) Shinya Tsukamoto.

Cast: Salary Man (Tomoro Taguchi), Girlfriend (Kei Fujiwara), Metal Fetishist (Shinya Tsukamoto).

The Set-Up: The salary man and his girlfriend accidentally run over a metal fetishist, and dump his body in the woods. The salary man and his girlfriend have sex. He later experiences/hallucinates his body being taken over by metal, his girlfriend being possessed, and the revenge of the metal fetishist.

The Hero: Given his actions, it's quite hard to see him as a hero, particularly when he develops a rather large drill bit in place of his penis; the metal fetishist is as bad, threatening to take over the world (as you do).

The Femme Fatale: The girlfriend is torn between horror, and being quite turned on by what she sees, but then she has (in a dream sequence?) buggered the salary man with a vacuum cleaner attachment she's just grown.

Playing The Angles: Not a film for the faint of stomach, the narrative I've given being far too linear compared to the actual experience of watching the film, which has flashbacks (forwards?), dream sequences and shifts points of view. It can be read as a literalization of the fear of being penetrated or penetrating, or an erotic of the artificial, or as the mad dream of a sick so-and-so. The game-over ending reminds us of computers (this is all a game? the characters are all cyborgs, programmed in some way?) and the fetishist is clearly a species of street life.

The Style: Black and white, at time stop-motion animated, with pantomime violence and a rich visceral love of metal.

The Pay-Off: The first time I saw this, they'd already ruined two prints trying to put subtitles on, so the cinema handed us copies of the script to read along to the Japanese. As such it made no sense whatsoever, and probably doesn't now. There's a sick kind of beauty to it, and it has to be seen to be believed. And even then maybe not.... *Tetsuo II: Bodyhammer* (1992), by the same director, is a long remake in colour and a kind of sequel. A third film, with a flying Tetsuo, has long been rumoured.

Terminator 2: Judgement Day (1991)

Director: James Cameron. Producer: James Cameron. Writers: James Cameron & William Wisher. Cinematographer: Adam Greenberg. Film Editors: Conrad Buff & Mark Goldblatt & Richard A Harris. Production Designer: Joseph Nemec III.

Cast: The Terminator (Arnold Schwarzenegger), Sarah Connor (Linda Hamilton), John Connor (Edward Furlong), T-1000 (Robert Patrick).

The Set-Up: A new model Terminator is sent back to kill Sarah's son, John, and a new version of the old Terminator is sent back to protect him. Sarah, confined to a mental hospital with persecution mania, takes some persuading that it is her friend, and has been building up her muscles. John, with Terminator in tow, sets out to survive the T-1000 and to prevent the development of Terminators in general. Can anyone spot the paradoxes here?

The Hero: A toss-up between the distinctly good guy Terminator and the spunky, punky, and (uh-oh) dangerously cute John. (What is it with sf movies and cute kids? Enough already!)

The Femme Fatale: Sarah Connor is a whole lot more fatal this time, but without a love interest.

Playing The Angles: After the rather bloodthirsty Terminator of the first film, this becomes a peace lover. After all, Freddy Krueger had mutated from child molester to wisecracking anti-hero to (in the form of Edward Scissorhands) tragic hero. And so the unstoppable killing machine becomes the father John never had, and is persuaded not to kill people. Just kneecap them. So that's OK then.

The Underworld: Again, preventing the hell of the future.

The Style: Explosions! Motorcycle chases! Melting characters! More explosions!

The Pay-Off: A big-budget follow-up, one of the most expensive films ever made, and a massive worldwide hit. LA's storm drains are shown to great effect, and Edward Furlong puts the punk back into cyberpunk. Plenty of violence on the mean streets, but sanitised.

The Lawnmower Man (1992)

Director: Brett Leonard. Producer: Gimel Everett. Writers: Brett Leonard & Gimel Everett. Cinematographer: Russell Carpenter. Film Editor: Alan Baumgarten. Production Designer: Alex McDowell.

Cast: Jobe Smith (Jeff Fahey), Doctor Lawrence Angelo (Pierce Brosnan).

The Set-Up: Angelo decides to upgrade the simpleton handyman Jobe's intelligence by hooking him up to some virtual reality and injecting him. Jobe develops unanticipated abilities, and is coveted by the military - Angelo's bosses. Jobe has other ideas though, and wishes vengeance on those who have mistreated him.

The Hero: Angelo is a scientist who bares his soul (and his chest) to an audio diary at various points. His heart is in the right place, as is his chest hair.

The Femme Fatale: There's a wife who leaves him early on.

Playing The Angles: The graphics of virtual reality are pretty, as are the effects when Jobe develops supernatural powers. But basically this is an updating of *Flowers For Algernon* (1966), with a *Frankenstein* spin. Jobe loses our sympathy, and his shirt, as it's payback time.

The Underworld: Jobe becomes the devil incarnate, virtual reality is a kind of spiritual or haunted realm, which ends up harrowing actual reality.

The Style: 1970s horror, plus military plotting and state-of-the-art (but finally meaningless) effects.

The Pay-Off: This is a film Stephen King sued to have his name removed from – with a faint whiff of a title of a short story he had written being taken as a reason to label it *Stephen King's The Lawnmower Man*. You can see his point though. There's a director's cut, restoring 40 minutes of lost material. Hold out for the shorter version. This, unbelievably, was a hit.

Armitage III: Poly-Matrix: The Movie (1994)

Director: Takuya Sato. Animation Directors: Kunihiro Abe & Hiroyuki Ochi. Writer: Chiaki Konaka.

Voices: Ross Sylibus (Kiefer Sutherland), Armitage (Elizabeth Berkley), D'Anclaude (Dan Woren).

The Set-Up: This film is an example of anime. Mars is an Earth colony, with type II robots doing the trivial work. As cop Sylibus arrives on Mars he witnesses a shoot-out between cop Armitage and D'Anclaude, who has killed a country music singer. The singer turns out to be a type III robot, one of a number which are being killed. Sylibus is partnered with Armitage to track down the killers, and soon realises that Armitage, too, is a type III...

The Hero: Sylibus' partner was killed by a cyborg, so he has no reason to like robots, but he himself has an artificial limb.

The Femme Fatale: Armitage looks like a young punk girl, with bra, stockings and suspenders, which is the standard costume for the female characters.

Playing The Angles: Clearly this becomes reminiscent of *Blade Runner*, which the big rainy city setting, Sylibus' developing romance with Armitage (which at the same time is a father/daughter relationship), the tough police boss, the break with procedure... The robots are hiding among people, for their own safety. In the end this seems to be a plea for tolerance, possibly among racial lines, as Earth-Mars politics are hurriedly grafted onto the plot. Could Armitage be a faint reference to a character to *Neuromancer*? Would it mean anything if it was?

The Pay-Off: Kiefer plays it more deadpan than Harrison Ford did in *Blade Runner*, which is to say in virtual monotone, and Elizabeth Berkely shows all the talent she did in *Showgirls* (1995). Nice set design, if slightly jerky animation. And no, you didn't miss the first two movies, III is a designation of a type of robot.

Johnny Mnemonic (1995)

Director: Robert Longo. Producer: Don Carmody. Writer: William Gibson. Cinematographer: François Protat. Film Editor: Ronald Sanders. Production Designer: Nilo Rodis-Jamero. Art Director: Dennis Davenport.

Cast: Johnny Mnemonic (Keanu Reeves), Jane (Dina Meyer), J-Bone (Ice-T), Takahashi (Takeshi Kitano), Street Preacher (Dolph Lundgren).

The Set-Up: Johnny has been hired to deliver computer information from Beijing to Newark, New Jersey, but they've overloaded the brain implant that he carries it in. And what's worse, the owners of the information, and the Japanese Mafia, the Yakuza, are after him, as is a cyborg preacher, and the three keys to unlock his brain have been scattered. He has 24 hours to clear his brain before he dies.

The Hero: Johnny has removed his childhood memories to make way for the implant, which is odd given the oft repeated claim in the real world that we only use about a tenth of our brains. Still, that wouldn't be so poignant. When he's not reeling from quasi-flashback, Johnny can more or less handle himself with a gun or any number of gadgets, and he's sure got a square jaw. Unfortunately, he clearly can't trust the company he works for. And unfortunately, he's played by Keanu Reeves – an adequate actor but here miscast.

The Femme Fatale: When we first meet Jane she is a wannabe bodyguard, with some kind of implants, but not quite fast enough to get a job. She has grown up on the streets, and knows her way around. As the film progresses, she starts losing the make-up and the futuristic look.

Playing The Angles: The information relates to a medical corporation named Pharmakon (which may be a reference to philosopher Jacques Derrida's discussion of the word Pharmakon in Plato, meaning both 'poison' and 'cure' – or then again, maybe it isn't), who should be a big player in a world ravaged by a new kind of plague. Johnny, meanwhile, narrowly escapes a virus.

The Style: At first the future seems quite convincing, but crowded streets give way to strangely deserted backstreets, daft camera angles, and some really dodgy matte shots. The subliminal footage intercut with computer-generated materials is pretty enough to look at. Johnny, like all action heroes of the 1990s, is given oh-so-witty one-liners to deliver, to prove how cool and hip he is. Unfortunately Keanu fails to deliver virtually any of them with the required degree of coolness and, er, hipness.

The Underworld: An AI who is a recurring character is the avatar of a dead person, and Johnny seems to be flooded with memories of a flooded childhood.

The Pay-Off: At first I really thought that this was an underrated film, conveniently ignoring the lazy cliché of the scrolling infodump at the start setting up the narrative. In the background in one scene there is even a Bogart movie playing, probably *The Maltese Falcon*, in homage to cyberpunk's origins. And the early action is well handled. But as the film progresses it seems to lose its way, and the acting becomes more wooden and stilted as Jane takes a larger rôle. Dolph Lundgren is ridiculous, and Henry Rollins as a doctor with a heart is well out of his depth. Reeves in the right rôle is a revelation – but this is clearly not it.

Kokaku Kidotai/Ghost In The Shell (1995)

Director: Mamoru Oshii. Producers: Mitsuhisa Ishikawa & Ken Iyadomi & Yoshimasa Mizuo & Shigeru Watanabe. Writer: Kazunori Itô. Cinematographer: Hisao Shirai. Film Editor: Shuichi Kakesu. Production Designer: Takashi Watabe. Art Director: Hiromasa Ogura.

Cast: Major Motoko Kusanagi (Atsuko Tanaka/Mimi Woods), Bateau (Akio Ôtsuka/Richard George), Aramaki (Tamio Oki /William Frederick).

The Set-Up: The security forces use cyborgs as agents, and cyborgs Kusanagi and Bateau get caught up in investigating infiltration into intergovernmental negotiations. Someone seems to be hacking into cyborgs and taking control, and they want to track down the puppet master. Unfortunately, someone else wants him (or her) as well.

The Hero: Bateau is played (in the English version at least) as the downbeat, exhausted cop, with no life outside his work.

The Femme Fatale: Kusanagi is more prone to introspection, worrying about the loss of her own identity. She is a dab hand with weapons, and athletic with it.

Playing The Angles: The line from *Corinthians* about seeing through a glass darkly (so beloved by Philip K Dick) is here repeated, but taken as a comment on personal evolution rather than levels of reality. The final climactic shoot-out takes place in a Natural History museum, with first dinosaur skeletons and then a diagram of evolution being destroyed. The next stage is to leave the meat behind, or rather not to get too attached to any given body.

The Underworld: The body is something to be transcended, just a stage in the transmigration of souls – all that remains of the humanity of Bateau and Kusanagi is a ghost, a ghost which may be haunted in turn.

The Style: Based on a manga, the animation is a mix of traditional and computer animation, with some remarkable cityscape backgrounds. Like in parts of *Blade Runner*, the narrative often pauses to take in the scenery.

The Pay-Off: Cyberpunk as police procedural, with musing on identity in a reprogrammable cyborg world.

Strange Days (1995)

Director: Kathryn Bigelow. Producers: James Cameron & Steven-Charles Jaffe. Writers: James Cameron & Jay Cocks. Cinematographer: Matthew F Leonetti. Film Editor: Howard Smith. Production Designer: Lilly Kilvert. Art Director: John Warnke.

Cast: Lenny Nero (Ralph Fiennes), Lornette 'Mace' Mason (Angela Bassett), Faith Justin (Juliette Lewis), Max Peltier (Tom Sizemore).

The Set-Up: It is the eve of the new millennium (well, no, actually, it's the end of 1999) and Lenny Nero traffics in virtual experiences, which viewers experience via a skullcap. When he receives a disc of the murder of his old friend Ivy, who had tried to contact him earlier in the day, and who we know was on the run from the cops, he fears for the safety of his ex-girlfriend Faith. Enlisting the help of ex-cop Max, who is already following Faith, and personal security expert Macey, he tries to protect her and uncover what Ivy was trying to tell him.

The Hero: Lenny is an ex-cop, turned greaseball in leather. He is snide, whiny, and over self-assured for someone who gets beaten up so often. But he is one of the good guys, and it's not his fault if he's being played for a sucker.

The Femme Fatale: Mace has ample abilities, and can defend herself with a gun or her bare hands. She refuses to have anything to do with the playbacks, preferring reality to repeats. Quite why is not explained, but you can see her point. Faith, meanwhile, has attitude, and is not going to go back to Lenny simply because she's in danger.

Playing The Angles: The millennium is just there to crank up the apocalyptic tension, as LA seems to be a simultaneous party and riot, with police and tanks on the streets. Behind all the murders is a post-Rodney King LA, and the racism of some of the characters and the underlying narrative is echoed in an interracial love affair of the two leads. With a murder-mystery thriller there is a sharp indictment of modern-day America.

The Style: Bigelow's trademarks are on show: notably her taste for night shoots, and the fetish for smoky blue light (plus red on occasions) cutting through it. Her films are known for their testosterone count, and this is no exception.

The Underworld: This is Hell, nor are we out of it.

The Pay-Off: I'm not convinced the various plots weld together in the end, but given the explanation is shown in about 50 shots it's easy to miss something. The deus ex machina of an elderly white male police commissioner is touchingly naïve, and the audience satisfying retribution on two of the villains avoids the more apocalyptic vision of a race riot that would do good as it burnt LA. But still, an impressive work for Hollywood.

Dark City (1998)

Director: Alex Proyas. Writers: Alex Proyas & David S Goyar & Lem Dobbs. Producers: Andrew Mason & Alex Proyas. Cinematographer: Dariusz Wolski. Film Editor: Dov Hoenig. Production Designers: George Liddle & Patrick Tatopoulos. Art Directors: Richard Hobbs & Michelle McGahey.

Cast: John Murdoch (Rufus Sewell), Dr Daniel Paul Schreber (Kiefer Sutherland), Emma Murdoch/Anna (Jennifer Connelly), Inspector Frank Bumstead (William Hurt).

The Set-Up: John Murdoch awakes in a hotel bath, uncertain of his name or identity, and runs after having being rung by the psychiatrist Dr Schreber. A body is found in the room, and Murdoch is suspected of murder. John finds his way to his wife, and narrowly avoids arrest. All he has to do is continue to do so whilst also avoiding the nasty pale people and working out why it is always dark and why everyone else falls asleep at midnight.

The Hero: Murdoch begins by looking confused and vulnerable, but he has hidden talents not even he knows about and that the script never bothers to explain.

The Femme Fatale: Emma Murdoch is his wife, or thinks she is, and has had an affair that he now knows about – except he's clearly forgotten. I think. She's a singer in a night-club, and goes to the police to help them find him.

Playing The Angles: There are these aliens, the Strangers, who are a dying race, and who have assembled a zoo of humans in an artificial environment to observe their behaviour and find out what makes them human. Having observed them in one situation, the Strangers have the city rearranged, and inject people with new memories. The film seems to make some distinction between mental memories and the heart, but doesn't seem to demonstrate this. Murdoch seems to have acquired the power to rearrange things as well.

The Style: It's a city, it's dark. There's a sense of the 40s about the architecture and the costumes, although William Hurt plays it as if he's just been playing William Lee in Cronenberg's *Naked Lunch* (1992). Which amounts to the same thing, come to think of it. The Strangers are refugees from Magritte's paintings of businessmen. The city operates at various levels, with elevated railways and roads, lots of back alleys and staircases. One odd and disconcerting aspect of the film is the music by Trevor Jones: it's playing virtually constantly throughout the film at a very low level, little more than a rumble of brass instruments. It adds to the rather depressed tone of the whole.

The Pay-Off: There's some dodgy model work that doesn't work on the small screen, although I seem to remember it was fine in a cinema. The conceptual breakthrough when we get our first glimpse out of the city (aside from almost subliminal sequences of memories) is a masterpiece, which again looks like dodgy matting on a second viewing. Overall the film is an odd generic hybrid (sf, horror, vampires, noir, police procedural) that doesn't *quite* work – it's scuppered perhaps by a degree of pomposity, Kiefer Sutherland's silly voice, and an unavoidable memory that the sinister Mr Hand is really that guy off the telly who used to do *The Crystal Maze*.

Lola Rennt/Run Lola Run (1998)

Director & Writer: Tom Tykwer. Producer: Stefan Arndt. Director Of Photography: Frank Griebe. Editor: Mathilde Bonnefoy. Set Designer: Alexander Manasse.

Cast: Lola (Franka Potente), Manni (Moritz Bleibtreu), Lola's father (Herbert Knaup).

The Set-Up: Lola's boyfriend has left a large amount of money on a subway train, and Lola only has 20 minutes to get that amount of money to the criminals he owes it to. Lola could try her father, who runs a bank, or try to gamble it, or track down the tramp who is now considerably richer than before. If at first you don't succeed...

The Hero: Manni is a bit of a fool, especially for wandering off without the money, but we all have our off days.

The Femme Fatale: Lola is red-haired, tattooed and good at running, which is what you need in a film called *Run Lola Run*. And if she doesn't get what she wants, she can scream and scream and scream until all the glass shatters.

Playing The Angles: The three attempts at getting the money demonstrate different possible futures, some fail, some succeed, some lead to death, some to life. Sometimes that large pane of glass survives, sometimes the van drives through it. Each of the three sequences begins with Lola running down stairs as a cartoon character or a character from a computer game, using up her lives.

The Style: Fast, frantic, frenetic, with a pulsing techno track.

The Underworld: People don't stay dead for long enough…

The Pay-Off: Low budget and high concept, an entertaining enough thriller that is instantly disposable. Still neat though. The what-if device of a few seconds' difference allows us to then follow the future of the people we see briefly, to find out what happens next. Pointless but neat.

eXistenZ (1999)

Director & Writer: David Cronenberg. Producers: David Cronenberg & Andras Hamori & Robert Lantos. Cinematographer: Peter Suschitzky. Film Editor: Ronald Sanders. Production Designer: Carol Spier. Art Director: Tamara Deverell.

Cast: Allegra Geller (Jennifer Jason Leigh), Ted Pikul (Jude Law), Kiri Vinokur (Ian Holm), Gas (Willem Dafoe).

The Set-Up: The leading game designer, Allegra Geller, is testing her new game eXistenZ with a focus group when she is attacked by a gun-wielding fanatic. She escapes with Ted Pikul and holes up in a motel. Her pod, the organic computer which she uses, and which has the only copy of her game on it (has she never heard of back-ups?) is ill. She persuades Ted to test it out, only he hasn't got a gameport in his spine which enables him to use the pod, and getting one could mean blowing their cover, not to say inconveniencing an already very worried Ted.

The Hero: Ted tries to do his best, but it doesn't seem to be good enough.

The Femme Fatale: Allegra is a tough cookie who doesn't suffer fools and lives for her pod.

Playing The Angles: Cronenberg was inspired by the plight of Salman Rushdie when he started writing the film, but the tale of the threatened artist mutated to a play on realities: how do Ted and Allegra know they're not still in the game when the assassin appears? How do we know that focus group wasn't part of the game? How do you know that reading this book is not part of the game? How do I know that I don't need to go and lie down in a darkened room right now?

The Style: Visceral, being David Cronenberg. All the technology looks organic, especially the computers and the guns.

The Pay-Off: *Videodrome*-lite is an unfair characterisation (if only to *Videodrome*), but there's the sense that we've seen this film before, and that the reality games are by the numbers. As if to note his nod to the master of shuffling realities, Philip K Dick, Cronenberg has his characters eat from Perky Pat takeaways, Perky Pat being a character in a Dick short story ('The Days Of Perky Pat') and a novel *The Three Stigmata Of Palmer Eldritch*. Still, no one does organic quite like Cronenberg.

The Matrix (1999)

Directors & Writers: The Wachowski Brothers. Producer: Joel Silver. Cinematographer: Bill Pope. Film Editor: Zach Staenberg. Production Designer: Owen Paterson. Art Directors: Hugh Bateup & Michelle McGahey.

Cast: Thomas A Anderson/Neo (Keanu Reeves), Morpheus (Laurence Fishburne), Trinity (Carrie-Anne Moss), Agent Smith (Hugo Weaving).

The Set-Up: International terrorist Morpheus is seeking the One, who turns out to be the hacker and software worker Thomas A Anderson, aka Neo (note the anagram). Before he can make contact, Neo is taken into custody by Agent Smith and fitted with a bug. Trinity, a veteran hacker, removes it, and takes him to meet Morpheus, who explains that the world which surrounds them is a fake, the Matrix, which is an illusion to keep humanity happy whilst it is being stored in vats to power the machines, computers and AIs that now runs the world. Neo's mission, should he choose to accept it, is to reveal the truth to the world and defeat the Agents, the AI software policemen who patrol the Matrix.

The Hero: Keanu is skilled at the vacancy that much of the rôle demands – disbelief that his computer is a channel for someone to contact him, that someone can help him down the telephone, that the truth is out there. And he buffs up pretty well for the shades and long cloak that the fighting demands later in the film.

The Femme Fatale: Trinity's leather and PVC are de rigueur for this kind of rôle, which has more than a touch of Gibson's Molly about her. She is a great hacker of the past, able to defend herself, and no doubt would put Neo right should he get the wrong signals from her. Alas, Hollywood narrative dictates that she fall in love with someone who is supposedly her junior, and snogs him at a crucial point. On the other hand, she does insist on going along on the dangerous missions, learns to pilot a helicopter (OK, so it's via a software download, but it's still action) and can operate a machine gun.

Playing The Angles: Which is better, the delusion of everyday life (which bears an uncanny likeness to Sydney) or the truth of living in the drains of a blasted city? The matrix world seems real enough from the start, albeit, the dark, rainy city that is associated with sf, post *Blade Runner*. As the film progresses, it leaves the clichés of noir behind and offers a sunnier side to the virtuality. (A particularly amusing sequence is towards the start, when the Agents arrive to take charge of the arrest of Trinity. The chief of police, who naturally supervises all such arrests personally, figures that two teams are sufficient to take one little woman. Kick butt action ensues. Cool.)

The Style: Noirish to start with, and then into John Woo territory of choreographed mayhem, bullets spat out all over, wire works, cloaks floating, unlikely stunts, and the remarkable special effect which enables us to pan around an object in mid flight. Keanu's range is never particularly wide, here or elsewhere, but Laurence Fishburne is also muted in a rôle that has exposition written all over it. Agent Smith also speaks in a strange tone, emphasising oddly, partly to indicate his artificial status as AI construct, and partly one suspects to disguise the fact that this was the fine actor last seen and heard in *The Adventures Of Priscilla, Queen Of The Desert* (1994).

The Underworld: The Matrix is the underworld, a world of shared dreams. The film could almost be Gnostic in its depiction of the sense that the real world is elsewhere from the prison of everyday life.

The Pay-Off: Prior to this, the writers/directors had made a neo-noir money-in-the-suitcase caper, *Bound* (1996), distinguished from all the others by placing two lesbians at the heart of the narrative. Here an intelligent script, perfect casting, and amazing camera work ensures that this is the best version of cyberpunk yet to make it to the screen. At the same time it's got to be noted how much is left undone: any portrayal of the last human city, Zion, any meeting with the real AIs behind it all, and the awakening of the rest of humanity. Two back-to-back sequels are promised. Cool.

7. Resource Materials

Books
Cyberpunk

Baird, Wilhelmina. *Chaos Come Again* (New York: Ace, 1996).

    ClipJoint (New York: Ace, 1994; Harmondsworth, Middlesex: Roc, 1996).

    CrashCourse (New York: Ace, 1993; Harmondsworth, Middlesex: Roc, 1995).

    PsyKosis (New York: Ace, 1995).

Bear, Greg. *Blood Music* (New York: Arbor House, 1985; London: Gollancz Vista, 1998).

    Queen Of Angels (London: Gollancz, 1990; New York: Warner, 1990).

    Slant (London: Legend, 1997; New York: Tor, 1997).

Bethke, Bruce. 'Cyberpunk'. *Amazing* (November, 1983).

    Headcrash (New York: Warner Aspect, 1995; London: Orbit, 1995).

Cadigan, Pat. *Dirty Work* (Shingletown, CA: Mark V Zeising, 1993).

    Fools (New York: Bantam Spectra, 1992; London: HarperCollins, 1994).

    Home By The Sea (Baltimore: WSFA Press, 1992).

    Mindplayers (New York: Bantam Spectra, 1987; London: Gollancz, 1988).

    Patterns (Jackson City, Kansas: Ursus, 1989; London: Grafton, 1991).

    Synners (London: HarperCollins, 1991; New York: Bantam Spectra, 1991).

    Tea From An Empty Cup (London: Voyager, 1998; New York: Tor, 1998).

    The Web: Avatar (London: Dolphin, 1999).

Cadigan, Pat, Fowler, Karen Joy & Murphy, Pat. *Letters From Home* (London: The Women's Press, 1991).

Egan, Greg. *Axiomatic* (London: Millennium, 1995; New York: Harperprism, 1997).

    Diaspora (London: Orion, 1997; New York: Harperprism, 1998).

    Distress (London: Millennium, 1995; New York: Harperprism, 1997).

    Luminous (London: Millennium, 1998).

    Permutation City (London: Millennium, 1994; New York: Harperprism, 1995).

    Quarantine (London: Legend, 1992; New York: Harperprism, 1995).

    Teranesia (London: Orion, 1999; New York: Harperprism, 1999).

Gibson, William. *Burning Chrome* (London: Gollancz, 1986; New York: Arbor House, 1986).

    Count Zero (London: Gollancz, 1986; New York: Arbor House, 1986).

Idoru (Harmondsworth, Middlesex: Viking, 1996; New York: Putnam's, 1996).

Mona Lisa Overdrive (London: Gollancz, 1988; New York: Bantam Spectra, 1988).

Neuromancer (London: Gollancz, 1984; New York: Ace, 1984).

Virtual Light (Harmondsworth, Middlesex: Penguin, 1993).

Grimwood, Jon Courtenay. *Lucifer's Dragon* (London: NEL, 1998).

neoAddix (London: NEL, 1997).

redRobe (London: Earthlight, 2000).

reMix (London: Earthlight, 1999).

Ings, Simon. *Headlong* (London: HarperCollinsVoyager, 1999).

Hot Head (London: Grafton, 1992).

Hotwire (London: HarperCollins, 1995).

Jones, Gwyneth. *Escape Plans* (London: Unwin, 1986).

Kairos (London: Unwin Hyman, 1988; London: Gollancz, 1995).

Kadrey, Richard. *Covert Culture Sourcebook* (New York: St Martin's Press, 1993).

Kamikaze L'Amour (New York: St Martin's Press, 1995).

Metrophage (London: Gollancz, 1988; New York: Ace, 1988).

Laidlaw, Marc. *Dad's Nuke* (New York: Fine, 1985; London: Gollancz, 1986).

Kalifornia (New York: St Martin's Press, 1993).

Neon Lotus (New York: Bantam Spectrum, 1988).

The Orchid Eater (New York: St Martin's Press, 1994).

Lewitt, Shariann. *Momento Mori.* (New York: Tor, 1995).

Maddox, Tom. *Halo* (London: Legend, 1991; New York: Tor, 1991).

Newman, Kim. *The Night Mayor* (London: Simon And Schuster, 1989; New York: Carroll & Graf, 1989).

Noon, Jeff. *Automated Alice* (London: Doubleday, 1996; New York: Crown, 1996).

Needle In The Groove (London: Anchor, 2000).

Nymphomation (London: Doubleday, 1997).

Pixel Juice: Stories From The Avant Pulp (London: Doubleday, 1998).

Pollen (Greater Manchester: Ringpull, 1995; New York: Crown, 1996).

Vurt (Littleborough: Ringpull, 1993; New York: Crown, 1995).

Piercy, Marge. *He, She And It* (New York: Knopf, 1991)

Body Of Glass (Harmondsworth, Middlesex: Michael Joseph, 1992).

Rucker, Rudy. *Freeware* (New York: Avon, 1997).

Realware (New York: Eos, 2000).

Software (New York: Ace, 1982).

Transreal! (Englewood, Co. : WCS Books, 1991).

Wetware (New York: Avon, 1988; London: NEL, 1989).

White Light (London: Virgin, 1980; New York: Ace, 1980).

Shiner, Lewis. *Deserted Cities Of The Heart* (London: Abacus, 1988; New York: Doubleday Foundation, 1988).

Frontera (New York: Baen, 1984; London: Sphere, 1985).

Shirley, John. *City Come A-Walkin'* (New York: Ace, 1980).

Eclipse (New York: Bluejay, 1985; London: Methuen, 1986).

Eclipse Corona (New York: Popular Library Questar, 1990).

Eclipse Penumbra (New York: Popular Library Questar, 1988).

The Exploded Heart (Asheville NC: Eyeball Books, 1996).

Heatseeker. Foreword By Stephen Brown. (Los Angeles: Scream Press, 1989; London: Grafton, 1990).

Stephenson, Neal. *Cryptonomicon* (London: William Heinemann, 1999; New York: Avon, 1999).

The Diamond Age (Harmondsworth, Middlesex: Viking, 1995; New York: Bantam Spectra, 1995).

In The Beginning ... Was The Command Line (New York: Avon, 1999).

Snow Crash (New York: Bantam Spectra, 1992; Harmondsworth, Middlesex: Roc, 1993).

Zodiac: The Eco-Thriller (New York: Atlantic Monthly, 1988; London: Bloomsbury, 1988).

Stephenson, Neal & George, J Frederick writing as Stephen Bury. *Interface: A Novel* (New York: Bantam, 1994).

Sterling, Bruce. *The Artificial Kid* (New York: Harper & Row, 1980; Harmondsworth, Middlesex: Penguin, 1985).

Crystal Express (Sauk City, Wi.: Arkham House, 1989; London: Legend, 1990).

Distraction (New York: Bantam Spectra, 1998; London: Millennium, 1999).

Globalhead (London: Millennium, 1992; Shingletown CA: Mark V. Zeising, 1992).

The Hacker Crackdown: Law And Disorder On The Electronic Frontier (New York: Bantam, 1992; Harmondsworth, Middlesex: Penguin, 1994).

Heavy Weather (London: Millennium, 1994; New York: Bantam Spectra, 1994).

Holy Fire (London: Orion, 1996; New York: Bantam Spectra, 1996).

Islands In The Net (London: Legend, 1988; New York: Morrow/Arbor House, 1988).

Schismatrix (New York: Arbor House, 1985; Harmondsworth, Middlesex: Penguin, 1986).

Schismatrix Plus (Ace: New York, 1996).

Sterling, Bruce, ed. *Mirrorshades: The Cyberpunk Anthology* (London: Paladin, 1988; New York: Ace, 1988).

Womack, Jack. *Ambient* (London: Weidenfeld & Nicholson, 1987; London: Unwin, 1989).

    Elvissey (London: HarperCollins, 1993; New York: Tor, 1993).

    Heathern (London: Unwin Hyman, 1990; New York: Tor, 1990).

    Let's Put The Future Behind Us (New York: Atlantic Monthly Press, 1996; London: Flamingo, 1997).

    Random Acts Of Senseless Violence (London: HarperCollins, 1993; New York: Atlantic Monthly Press, 1994).

    Terraplane (London: Weidenfeld & Nicholson, 1988; New York: Tor, 1988).

Other Books Mentioned In Introduction

Aldiss, Brian. *Report On Probability A* (London & Boston: Faber & Faber, 1968).

Ballard, J G *The Atrocity Exhibition* (London: Jonathan Cape, 1970).

    Crash (London: Cape, 1973; New York: Farrar, Straus And Giroux, 1973).

Bester, Alfred. *The Stars My Destination* (New York: Signet, 1957).

    Tiger! Tiger! (London: Sidgwick & Jackson, 1956).

Blaylock, James. *Homunculus* (New York: Ace, 1986; London: Grafton, 1988).

    Lord Kelvin's Machine (Sauk City, Wi.: Arkham House, 1992; London: Grafton, 1993)

Brunner, John. *The Jagged Orbit* (New York: Ace, 1969; London: Sidgwick & Jackson, 1970).

    The Sheep Look Up (Harper And Row: New York, 1972; London: Dent, 1974).

    The Shockwave Rider (New York: Harper And Row, 1975; London: Dent, 1975).

    Stand On Zanzibar (Garden City, New York: Doubleday, 1968; London: Macdonald & Co, 1969).

Burgess, Anthony. *A Clockwork Orange* (London: Heinemann, 1962; New York: W W Norton, 1963).

Burroughs, William S. *Naked Lunch* (Paris: Olympia Press, 1959; London: John Calder, 1964).

    The Wild Boys: A Book Of The Dead (New York: Grove, 1971; London: Calder and Boyars, 1972).

Delany, Samuel R. *Babel-17* (New York: Ace, 1966; London: Sphere, 1967).

    Dhalgren (New York: Bantam, 1975; London: Grafton: 1992).

Dick, Philip K. *Do Androids Dream Of Electric Sheep?* (Garden City, New York: Doubleday, 1968; London: Rapp & Whiting 1969).

    Vulcan's Hammer (New York: Ace, 1960; London: Arrow, 1976).

Jeter, K W. *Dr Adder*. Afterword By Philip K Dick (New York: Bluejay, 1984; London: Grafton, 1987).

Infernal Devices (New York: St Martin's Press, 1987; London: Grafton, 1988).

Morlock Night (New York: DAW, 1979; London: Grafton, 1989).

Le Guin, Ursula. *The Left Hand Of Darkness* (London: Macdonald & Co, 1969; New York: Ace, 1969).

MacLeod, Ken. *The Cassini Division* (London: Orbit, 1998; New York: Tor, 1999).

The Sky Road (London: Orbit, 1999).

The Star Fraction (London: Orbit, 1995).

The Stone Canal (London: Orbit, 1996; New York: Tor, 2000).

McAuley, Paul J. *Fairyland* (London: Gollancz, 1995; New York: Avon, 1996).

Powers, Tim. *The Anubis Gates* (New York: Ace, 1983; London: Chatto and Windus, 1985).

Russ, Joanna. *Alyx* (Boston: Gregg Press, 1976); *The Adventures Of Alyx* (London: The Women's Press, 1985).

The Female Man (New York: Bantam, 1975; London: Star, 1977).

Picnic On Paradise (New York: Ace, 1968; London: Macdonald & Co, 1969).

Shelley, Mary. *Frankenstein, Or The Modern Prometheus* (London: Lackington, Hughes, Harding, Mavor & Jones, 1818).

Spinrad, Norman. *Bug Jack Barron* (New York: Walker, 1969; London: Macdonald, 1970).

Tiptree Jr, James. 'The Girl Who Was Plugged In' in *New Dimensions 3*. Edited by Robert Silverberg (New York: Nelson Doubleday, 1973).

Wells, H G. *The Time Machine, An Invention* (London: William Heinemann, 1895).

Non-Fiction On Cyberpunk

Bukatman, Scott. *Blade Runner* (London: BFI, 1997).

Terminal Identity: The Virtual Subject In Post-Modern Science Fiction (Durham and London: Duke University Press, 1993).

Cavallaro, Dani. *Cyberpunk And Cyberculture : Science Fiction And The Work Of William Gibson* (London: Athlone, 2000).

Dery, Mark. *Escape Velocity* (London: Hodder and Stoughton, 1996).

ed. *Flame Wars: The Discourse Of Cyberculture* (Durham and London: Duke University Press, 1994).

Featherstone, Mike & Burrows, Roger. *Cyberspace/Cyberbodies/Cyberpunk: Cultures Of Technological Embodiment* (New York: Sage, 1996).

Gray, Chris Hables, ed. *The Cyborg Handbook* (London and New York: Routledge, 1995).

Hayles, N Katherine. *How We Became Post-human* (Chicago and London: University of Chicago Press, 1999).

Kernan, Judith B, ed. *Retrofitting Blade Runner* (Bowling Green, OH: Bowling Green State University Popular Press, 1991).

Olsen, Lance. *William Gibson* (Mercer Island: Starmont, 1992).

Sammon, Paul M. *Future Noir: The Making Of Blade Runner* (New York and London: HarperCollins, 1996; London: Orion Media, 1996).

Slusser, George & Shippey, Tom, eds. *Fiction 2000: Cyberpunk And The Future Of Narrative* (Athens, Ge: University of Georgia Press, 1992).

Springer, Claudia. *Electronic Eros* (Austin: University of Texas Press, 1996).

Videos & DVDs

Akira
PAL format video, Dubbed, Catalogue Number: IWCV1001
PAL format video, Subtitled, Catalogue Number: IWCV1002, incl making of
Armitage III: Poly-Matrix: The Movie
NTSC format video, Dubbed, ASIN: 6304586450
Blade Runner
NTSC format video, Widescreen, Special Edition, ASIN: 6305363668
PAL format video, Catalogue Number: S070008
PAL format video, Director's Cut, Widescreen, Catalogue Number: S012682
Region 1 Director's Cut, Widescreen, ASIN: 0790729628
Region 2 DVD, Director's Cut, Widescreen, Catalogue Number: D012905
Region 2 DVD, Director's Cut II, Catalogue Number: MTD2000
Dark City
NTSC format video, ASIN: 0780622545
NTSC format video, Widescreen, ASIN: 078062551X
PAL format video, Catalogue Number: EVS1276
Region 1 DVD, Widescreen, ASIN: 0780622553
Region 2 DVD, Catalogue Number: EDV9005
eXistenZ
NTSC format video, ASIN: 6305538018
PAL format video, Catalogue Number: AA019S
Region 1 DVD, Widescreen, ASIN: B00000K31V
Region 2 DVD, Widescreen, Catalogue Number: AA019DVD
Johnny Mnemonic
NTSC format video, ASIN: B00000GLDC
PAL format video, Catalogue Number: 8907BD
Region 1 DVD, Widescreen, ASIN: 0767802454
Kokaku Kidotai/Ghost In The Shell
NTSC format video, Dubbed, ASIN: 6304083769
NTSC format video, Subtitled, ASIN: 6304083777
NTSC format video, special edition, Dubbed, ASIN: 6304539487

NTSC format video, special edition, Subtitled ASIN: 6304539495

PAL format video, with making of, Subtitled, Catalogue Number: MANV1169

PAL format video, Dubbed, Catalogue Number: MANV1133

Region 1 DVD, Widescreen, with making of, ASIN: 6304493681

Region 2 DVD, Subtitled, Catalogue Number: MANG5529

The Lawnmower Man

NTSC format video, ASIN: 6302483395

Region 1 DVD, Widescreen, ASIN: 6304604572

Region 2 DVD, Director's Cut, Widescreen, Catalogue Number: VAD10008

Lola Rennt/Run Lola Run

NTSC format video, Dubbed in English, ASIN: B000021Y75

NTSC format video, Subtitled, ASIN: B000021Y74

PAL format video, Subtitled, Catalogue Number: CVR29501

Region 1 DVD, Widescreen, ASIN: B000021Y77

Region 2 DVD, Catalogue Number: CDR29501

Strange Days

NTSC format video, ASIN: 630398021X

NTSC format video, Widescreen, ASIN: 6304432453

PAL format video, Catalogue Number: 0448863

Region 1 DVD, Widescreen, ASIN: B00000JSJC

The Terminator

NTSC format video, ASIN: B00000JGEH

Terminator 2: Judgement Day

NTSC format video, ASIN: B00000JGEI

NTSC format video, Widescreen, ASIN: 6304126344

PAL format video, Catalogue Number: 0782503

Region 1 DVD, Widescreen, ASIN: 0784010188

Region 1 DVD, lots of extras, Widescreen, ASIN: B00004TRD8

Tetsuo: The Iron Man

All Regions DVD, ASIN: 6305077924

The Matrix

NTSC format video, Special Edition, ASIN: B00000K2SC

NTSC format video, Widescreen, Special Edition, ASIN: B00000K2SE

PAL format video, Catalogue Number: S016985

PAL format video, Widescreen, Catalogue Number: S017665

Region 1 DVD, Widescreen, Collector's Edition, ASIN: B00000K19E

Region 2 DVD, Widescreen, Catalogue Number: D017737

Videodrome

NTSC format video, ASIN: 6300182770

PAL format video, Catalogue Number: 0782983

Region 1 DVD, Widescreen, ASIN: 0783228457

Magazines

SF Eye: The magazine which perhaps most wholeheartedly embraced cyberpunk, and slipstream, and beyond cyberpunk. Publication was suspended indefinitely with issue 15, but back issues are available from *SF EYE*, PO Box 18539, Asheville, NC 28814, USA. E-mail: eyebrown@interpath.com. Web: http://www.empathy.com/eyeball/sfeye.html

Interzone: A magazine which began as a quarterly and is now monthly (the last monthly sf fiction magazine in the world, apparently). It published early stories by Gibson and Sterling, non-fiction by Sterling and a host of other goodies. Subscriptions details: Interzone, 217 Preston Drove, Brighton BN1 6FL, UK. E-mail: interzone@cix.co.uk. Web: http://www.sfsite.com/interzone/

Webpages

Greg Bear's homepage includes news, articles, interviews, radio transcripts, biographical details and information on how to order his books. http://www.gregbear.com/gregbear/bear.nsf

Bruce Bethke's homepage includes information on books, short fiction and non-fiction and his coining of the word cyberpunk. http://www.spedro.com/

Pat Cadigan's webpage, including publication details, reprints of articles, is designed and maintained by her husband. It also includes details of how to get hold of out-of-print titles by her. http://www.wmin.ac.uk/%7Efowlerc/patcadigan.html

Greg Egan's own webpage includes information on his existing and forthcoming work, reprints of articles, interviews, stories and so on. http://www.netspace.net.au/%7Egregegan/

Jon Courtenay Grimwood's page includes information on his work and reviews of various sf novels. http://www.j-cg.co.uk/

Simon Ings. Details of works, reprints of articles. http://www.fisheye.demon.co.uk/home.html

Gwyneth Jones' homepage includes vital statistics, information about her work and some reprints of non-fiction. http://www.homeusers.prestel.co.uk/dreamer/

Richard Kadrey's novel *Metrophage* is on-line. http://www.cyberpunkproject.org/lib/metrophage/

An extract from *Kamikaze L'Amour*, 'Horse Latitudes' is available on-line. http://www.intertext.com/v5n4/latitudes.html

Tom Maddox's homepage includes actual short stories, articles and his (out-of-print) novel, *Halo*, as well as information on privacy. http://home.pacbell.net/tmaddox/

The official Kim Newman page includes materials on his fiction. http://indigo.ie/~imago/newman.html

Details of Jeff Noon's *Cobralingus* are available from the publisher. http://www.codexbooks.co.uk/codex.html. www.jeffnoon.com is supported by Noon and contains a lot material about his works.

Justina Robson's homepage includes bibliographic and biographical material, as well as information on writing workshops and yoga. http://www.lula.co.uk/

The Rudy Rucker Homepage includes games, software, columns, as well as biographical material and information about his books. http://www.mathcs.sjsu.edu/faculty/rucker/

Lewis Shiner's own webpage includes news and details of novels (including review quotations), short stories and non-fiction as well as an autobiographical sketch. http://www.lewisshiner.com/

John Shirley has an official website with biography, bibliography, non-fiction reprints and ordering details http://www.darkecho.com/JohnShirley/

Neal Stephenson's *Cryptonomicon* has a page devoted to it, with some information about the rest of his work http://www.cryptonomicon.com/main.html

Cheap Truth, Bruce Sterling's pseudonymous fanzine, is available at various sites. Try: http://www.io.com/~ftp/usr/shiva/SMOF-BBS/cheap.truth/ or http://lonestar.texas.net/%7Edub/cheap.html

The Bruce Sterling On-line Index offers texts of many of Sterling's speeches, articles and interviews. http://lonestar.texas.net/%7Edub/newfront.html

Jack Womack has various columns on-line on cranks. http://www.eventhorizon.com/sfzine/commentary/

The Essential Library

If you've enjoyed this book why not try the following titles in the Pocket Essentials library? Each is £2.99 unless otherwise stated.

New This Month @ £3.99 each: **Philip K Dick** by Andrew M Butler
Cyberpunk by Andrew M Butler
Next Month @ £3.99 each: **Conspiracy Theories** by Robin Ramsay
Marilyn Monroe by Paul Donnelley

Also Available

Film: **Woody Allen** by Martin Fitzgerald
Jane Campion by Ellen Cheshire
Jackie Chan by Michelle Le Blanc & Colin Odell
Joel & Ethan Coen by John Ashbrook & Ellen Cheshire
David Cronenberg by John Costello (£3.99)
Film Noir by Paul Duncan
Terry Gilliam by John Ashbrook
Heroic Bloodshed edited by Martin Fitzgerald
Alfred Hitchcock by Paul Duncan
Krzysztof Kieslowski by Monika Maurer
Stanley Kubrick by Paul Duncan
David Lynch by Michelle Le Blanc & Colin Odell
Steve McQueen by Richard Luck
Brian De Palma by John Ashbrook
Sam Peckinpah by Richard Luck
Slasher Movies by Mark Whitehead (£3.99)
Vampire Films by Michelle Le Blanc & Colin Odell
Orson Welles by Martin Fitzgerald
TV: **Doctor Who** by Mark Campbell
Books: **Noir Fiction** by Paul Duncan

Available at all good bookstores, or send a cheque to: **Pocket Essentials (Dept CY), 18 Coleswood Rd, Harpenden, Herts, AL5 1EQ UK**. Please make cheques payable to 'Oldcastle Books.' Add 50p postage & packing for each book in the UK and £1 elsewhere.

US customers can send $5.95 plus $1.95 postage & packing for each book to: **Trafalgar Square Publishing, PO Box 257, Howe Hill Road, North Pomfret, Vermont 05053, USA**. tel: 802-457-1911, fax: 802-457-1913, e-mail: tsquare@sover.net

Customers worldwide can order online at **www.pocketessentials.com**, **www.amazon.com** and at all good online bookstores.